The miracle of real forgiveness

Tom Carpenter

Chance plays no part in any scheme,
It only happens the way you dream.
You see a world "out there" to change, only to find
It happened first within your mind.

References:

"A Course in Miracles"
Published by the Foundation for Inner Peace, 1976
Widely available on the Internet

"The Gifts of God"
Published by the Foundation for Inner Peace
www.acim.org

"Dialogue on Awakening"
Published by Carpenters Press
www.tomandlindacarpenter.com

Contact Information:

www.theforgivenessmovement.org
www.tomandlindacarpenter.com
www.facebook.com/TheForgivenessNetwork

This book is dedicated to my dear friend,
Robert Holden.
With much appreciation for his key help and
support in the birth of the Forgiveness Movement,
for his gift of the Happiness Projects and for being a
truly loving presence in our consciousness.

"Forgiveness paints a picture of a world
where suffering is over, loss becomes impossible
and anger makes no sense.
Attack is gone and madness has an end.
What suffering is now conceivable?
What loss can be sustained?
The world becomes a place of joy, abundance,
charity and endless giving.
It is now so like to Heaven that it quickly
is transformed into the light that it reflects.
And so the journey
that the Son of God began has ended
in the light from which he came."

ACIM WB-249.1

Table of Contents

Preface
You Are Not Who You Think You Are

Think for a moment what it would be like to go about your day with your mind filled only with happy and loving thoughts. Everyone you meet has a smile and a glow of happiness about them. There is no sickness, no hunger, no conflict or lack; no striving, no blame, no expectations, no time and no death. Peace has replaced fear everywhere in this world. There is no word to describe hate for all the reasons not to love are gone. This is our state of mind without the thought of sin. This is our world when there is no guilt to judge. This is where the miracle of real forgiveness will take us.

For most of us the world seems quite a different place than this. And most significantly, it appears to bear little relevance to what we would like it to be. But what we need to learn is that it is a state of mind before it is a place. It is our thoughts that have made it all that it seems to be, and so the world we see is ours to change.

We are not who we pretend we are; "individual" victims of a capricious world, disconnected and different from other beings, destined to alternate between happiness and suffering and ultimately left alone to die. We are not the bodies that seem to define us. Nor can we be known by our ego thoughts or the behavior that they spawn.

The world is not what it seems to be. It is not a place where things can happen to us against our will. It is a state of mind fundamentally dedicated to the belief there is something wrong with us, and the experience of being separate and different in every way. "Seeing is believing," is our motto, while it is just the opposite that is true. It is not possible to change what we *truly* are. But it is possible to *believe* as we choose and to experience the effects of those beliefs.

The irony is we think that we are something different than what we are because of a belief that isn't true—"born in sin" as our religions put it. Bad things seem to happen to us at random because we don't recognize that we have made this world from thoughts of guilt.

It is this belief in sin and separation that have made our world. And each time we choose to rely on some variation of these same thoughts, similar experiences arise again reinforcing that our misperception is true. This, in turn, leads to repeating these choices and perpetuating an endless loop of the same fearful experiences.

Recognizing this, it is easier to understand why the world appears to be the way we now see it. All the hatreds, lost happiness, mistrust and pain have become "normal," the "reality" of how things are. We don't question if the world should be the way it is, or if there is an alternative because it already illustrates what we think is true.

In truth, we are bound together as integral parts of a single Mind/Spirit. We share a single Cause and a unified consciousness—something we cannot change regardless of our beliefs. What we were created to be cannot be lost. Though mostly buried, there remains in our mind the awareness of this real truth about us. While separateness is still our dominant belief, we are actually now in the process of letting it go. Thought by thought, slowly, guided by an inner Awareness, in ways we are mostly unconscious of, we are opening our mind to a different awareness of who we are.

We say it is a miracle when something happens in our world that contradicts the laws of our belief. Forgiveness, used in the way we will describe, becomes the practice of demonstrating to ourselves that we want to love instead of hate. Forgiving what we have judged opens our mind to recognize a sense of union, and the effects of how that changes our world are miraculous indeed.

The Miracle Of Real Forgiveness is about letting go of our misperceptions of who we are and what the world is, opening our mind and heart to a different truth. It is about learning that peace and joy come from "connecting" to each other, not blaming or looking for ways to be special and different. It is about releasing the guilt that has hidden our "real" Self, and finding the freedom to love again.

Introduction
Reconnecting With Our Self

Each of us came to this world looking for something because we have long believed there was something missing in us. That we are all complete and part of one harmonious Creation has been lost to our awareness. What we think we look for is something that will enrich our lives in the world; make us smarter, richer and have better relationships. That, at least, is how it seems to a belief that looks "outside" itself for what it seems to lack. But nothing really will satisfy our longing until we realize it is the part of our Self we have disowned that leaves us now with the sense that something is missing. It is the part we have taught ourselves to call brother, or friend, or enemy—or God.

Reconnecting with this part of us will not be easy for we have made an entire universe dedicated to making everything look different and do "unacceptable" things that we might practice our well-honed art of Self deception. Moment to moment, in subtle and not so subtle ways, we reaffirm our desire—our need—to be separate.

Separateness is a way of life that seems to provide us with someone else we can make wrong for what we really believe is wrong with us. We have made a world of separate bodies to identify the differences between us so that we can pretend to hide our own guilt in the things they do. And we have been eminently successful, for you can find little doubt anywhere in our world that hate and fear appear to be well justified.

The purpose of this book is to suggest we have a choice for the kind of world we live in. Since time began, we have been perpetuating a hoax upon ourselves, living a life of uncertainty, at times of indescribable pain, of suffering, fear and an endless search for peace and love when, in truth, everything we need to live in happiness is within us right now.

Our story of a world seems real because we have felt a need to change what is true. We continue to forget because we practice living by the principles of our deception. But even as our mind *seemed* to split from the one Mind, there was a Presence of Truth that remained with us. When we learn to accept that Presence and ask for help, we build a "bridge" connecting us to that part of our Mind that *is* real and *is* true. There is a vision of a different world that is held there; one made by thoughts that do not deny our innocent Oneness, but bring it into a sharper focus. It is here we can recognize what we really have been searching for and begin to see our journey's end.

The goal of real forgiveness is to lead us to this truth of who and what we are. But just to say the "truth" has little meaning when that truth is so far removed from our perception. We see ourselves now as creatures of a world—a world that represents the attributes of what we *imagine* to be true. Forgiveness is the tool that allows us to change the intention of our thoughts from judgment to the purpose of joining. This, in turn, changes the entire purpose of the world, allowing it to become a mirror for feelings of peace and joy, instead of hate and fear.

Our practice of real forgiveness will release the judgments that seemed to separate us and so will eventually open the door to a different world where we can practice a kind of loving that reminds us of our Oneness and satisfies what we long for. This is really what we want. And this is where the movement of real forgiveness will take us.

The miracle of real forgiveness, as outlined in this book, is derived primarily from the principles taught in *A Course in Miracles*. Here, using language we are familiar with, Jesus speaks of the need for us to correct our perception. He says forgiveness is our function because that is the most effective means to correct the error in our thinking that sin is real and has seemed to make a separation exist between us. As each one forgives and accepts their own innocence, they offer the awareness of innocence to everyone. They then share the *unwillingness* to judge error in anyone.

Forgiveness is the process *A Course In Miracles* uses to deny the appearances of our "human" ego perception and to bring to our consciousness an alternative way to "see" and react to the world. It is a means, quite literally, to change our experience of the world to a place of peace and joy. I hope these pages are a stimulus to pursue more deeply or begin anew this profound and beautiful teaching.

Aside from what I have quoted directly from *ACIM*, much of what I have written here is what I have learned from my own association with Jesus, the author of the *Course*. We have been in dialogue since 1988, some of which has been previously published in our book, *"Dialogue on Awakening."**

We have set up a website called *The Forgiveness Movement,** as a forum where we can consciously join with others through the focus of "real forgiveness." Its purpose is to provide a structure for people around the world of every race and religion to join in holding the awareness that there is a real alternative to hate and conflict; to deprivation and suffering. It is our intention to demonstrate there is a loving way to deal with our differences and also heal what seems to be a wounded and failing environment.

Together we have the ability to move our world toward peace and happiness. We can let go of our defenses and our grievances. We carry both the darkness of our fears and the light of peace within our mind. The heart of the *Forgiveness Movement* is a Forgiveness Support Network, a joining of those who are ready to choose the light that makes peace possible and be an inspiration for others to do the same.

Until we have a fuller understanding of what real forgiveness is, the freedom it offers can be misperceived as a way to avoid dealing with pain and suffering, instead of being the means to heal it. Many ask how can we forgive genocide? How can we forgive torture, child abuse and starvation? These are questions for which I will suggest an answer that will bring a lasting peace to all the world. I hope to open our mind to another way of thinking that can end for all time the hatred and suffering in our individual and collective experience.

Everyone has an idea now of what forgiveness means to them. Our inner Guide will use them all to bring about the goal of revealing a forgiven and a peaceful world. *ACIM* teaches what "real" forgiveness is, and we will look in depth at what that means. But when I think about forgiveness in its simplest form, I am reminded of a line from my favorite Rumi poem:

> *"Out beyond ideas of right doing and wrong doing,*
> *there is a field. I will meet you there."*

If the prospect of this reunion resonates with you, welcome to the Forgiveness Movement and the miracle of real forgiveness.

---

* "Dialogue on Awakening"   See inside cover printing information

* "The Forgiveness Movement"   www.theforgivenessmovement.org

I

The Practice of Deception

The mind "sees" only what it perceives to be true. Our world is the experience of this seeing. Because what we perceive to be true is actually not true, the appearances of our world are very deceiving.

The body is the vehicle mind uses as the symbol of its belief that it is separate from other minds. Being "made" by mind, it has no function of its own. Its brain does not "think", its eyes and ears report only what mind directs.

What is real and true is eternal and changeless. Nothing in the world is either eternal or changeless and so the world as we see it should not be considered real or true. As long as we believe that the appearances of the world are real we make them true and continue to live our lives as though we were victims of the "laws" it would seem to dictate.

Our eternal Oneness is changeless and is the truth. To insure we could not become completely lost in our misperception, God placed the Holy Spirit in our mind to hold this awareness for us until we are ready to again accept it for ourselves. A miracle occurs when we choose this Vision instead of our ego's perception, for this choice over-turns the laws of the world. When we have accepted this truth to replace our ego "truth," what our mind "sees" changes, and so must our world then also change.

f

Forgiveness is a way of changing the mind's focus and intention. It thus begins to awaken the dreamer from the story he is telling of being a body in a world of differences. This is fundamentally necessary in order to remember the nature of our unified and limitless Self, yet it is also a willingness to think of ourselves and our world in a way that initially seems to have no justification. The idea of literally letting the "world" go seems to destroy the foundation of the "self" we have chosen to believe lives there.

When seen through the ego's belief, the thought of letting the world go appears to be sacrificing what sustains us. Yet the shift we are making through the forgiveness process will teach us that it is not the world we are experiencing anyway; it is our thoughts. And when we have discovered it is *only* our thoughts that can make us more happy and peaceful, we will not need to look to the world for what has never been there anyway.

We struggle now to find better ways to preserve and defend our separateness when what will really make us happy is releasing the defenses of our judgments and finding the freedom to join. We have long forgotten a fundamental principle of our Oneness: *Nothing exists until it is shared.* In Oneness, isolation is impossible. Lasting happiness is meaningless to one who looks for it "alone." What is love until it is freely given? *Forgiveness is a tool for this change because its practice results in joining.*

The miracle of real forgiveness is in discovering the freedom that comes with accepting that part of your Self you had previously condemned. It is learning that releasing a brother from "his" guilt is the same as releasing yourself from yours. We are parts of a single consciousness, inter-connected in our common story about sin and separation. Awakening alone would be like imagining one thought in our mind could change while the rest of them remained as they were.

It might then seem pointless to pursue our own awakening until "everyone" else is doing the same. This seems a perfectly "logical" conclusion from within the ego's perception that separateness is real. But separateness is not real and *anyone* pursuing the truth does so for *everyone*. It is not an exaggeration to compare the closeness of our own thoughts to the presence of our brother. We seem to exist in a world where it is impossible to imagine this kind of connection, even in our closest relationships.

This is the value of knowing of the existence of the Holy Spirit within our mind and our ability to call upon the awareness held there to replace our own perception. Here there is no deception to confuse us about what awakening is or how to surrender to it. But it is necessary that we not resist our brother's awakening happening along with our own, by not judging how it should happen or on whose "schedule" it must takes place.

Real forgiveness is the practice of expressing our willingness to accept the miracle of seeing differently. This cannot be fully appreciated until we have felt the freedom that comes when we dismiss entirely a judgment we have made. Judgments divide the mind against itself. They are familiar, may even feel necessary in the moment, but it is a strain upon the mind to condemn itself, or another, for it denies the harmony inherent in its "DNA."

Despite any worldly appearance, loving without reason is the most natural thing we do. Peace is our "normal" state of mind. Happiness is the "default" condition when guilt has been let go. This is the changeless reality that exists just below our unnatural attempts to be separate.

Exposing the myth of separateness is the miracle of forgiveness. Moving together to accept this gift is the purpose and function for *The Forgiveness Movement Network.*

II

Guilt: The Hidden Cause of Our Experience

For many lifetimes, in all cultures, we have struggled to find a sense of self-worth in this world. Our drive to improve ourselves, to measure our worth by what we accomplish is testament to the feeling that we are born incomplete.

The cause of this feeling that there is something missing, of the need to prove our self worth, is a guilt so deeply hidden, so "natural," it is unquestioned. It seems far more fitting to profess our ignorance and inabilities than our talents and loving instincts. When we look out at this world and see all the suffering we cause ourselves and one another, we long for a better world, but not knowing its true cause we don't know how to change it. We have misperceived that the causes of the world are *in* the world. However, it is our thoughts driven by our hidden guilt that are responsible for all the heartache and the hatred, the diseases as well as the "natural" disasters that appear to happen in our world.

We have used our feelings of guilt to create an image in our mind of who we think we are, replacing the reality of what God created us to be. Our world and all our experience in it has come about because of our attempt to re-create ourselves;

to make something real that is different from what God Is and what we, then, must Be as well. Trying to replace His Creation with our own vastly different creation is what has made us feel separate from our Creator, from our brothers who are also like God, and from our unity as well.

What we will learn as we come to accept that it is we who have made our world is that there is a very simple principle we can apply toward changing our thoughts that have made it: *Let forgiveness express our natural desire to love and replace our unnatural need to judge.* Without our feelings of guilt, there is nothing *to* judge and our desire to love is set free.

Undefended loving opens the mind to opportunities for a broader range of happy relationships beyond those sought to satisfy ego desires and needs. Judgment constricts mind's function to the ego's goals of separation. It severely restricts our mental health and also limits the body's ability to function without pain.

Our feelings of guilt are so ingrained they create an automatic expectation, or standard, of what *should* be true. Until we begin to consciously take responsibility for our thoughts, we do not recognize that what we really want is what we already have *when our mind is free of guilt.* The way we learn this is to practice expressing a *different* standard of what we want to be true through the choices we make. This is the purpose of forgiveness: consciously choosing to recognize that it is love we want to find, not guilt, and so make choices inspired by our desire to love instead of the ego's need to look for fault.

The world is always a reflection of how we see ourselves. It can be a peaceful experience or an endless variety of threats. In effect, this means that our behavior is based upon what we believe is true about us. If we feel badly about ourselves we will behave in a way that is unacceptable to others. But by discovering there is a way to find a different and a loving self, we will then present a loving self to the world and *find a loving world in return.*

If you doubt the role guilt plays in your self-image, ask yourself if you deserve to be happy at all times. Are you free of all worry about your finances and health? Do you always feel loved and loving towards others? Is it your natural inclination to accept someone, or to find something to criticize—show them some way they could improve? *It is normal and natural to always feel good and loving.* When we don't, then some other feeling seems more important. This is the role guilt plays.

Why is our guilt so pervasive? It begins with our belief that we are born in sin—that there is something innately wrong with us. We have made the world as the experience of this belief. We are told it was when "a tiny mad idea" entered the mind of God's Son that he momentarily lost the awareness of his true Self in the dream about his idea. We don't remember this, of course, and any speculation about it serves mostly to make real what has no substance outside the dream. What is important is to realize the idea was insane. *We have not changed, can not change, the nature of the Thought that created us what we are!*

Sin and guilt are a concept that should be treated lightly, like other fables and fairy tales. That is not easy to do when we feel the pain and suffering that comes from the physical experience of our belief that guilt is real. The greatest legacy that sin's misperception leaves, however, is that it robs us of the memory of what love is.

In the practice of forgiveness, our guilty judgments will disappear and be replaced by the grace of the God-created Self that they have hidden. This is a major shift in self-identity. It is neither a simple understanding nor a quick and easy exchange. We have believed in our sin and guilt for so long that the freedom offered by forgiveness is not always welcomed nor is it satisfying to the ego. But within each of us, within our consciousness there is still that eternal light of grace held by the Holy Spirit that quietly calls to us. And when we are ready to listen, our journey from guilt to the awareness of Love's Presence will begin.

The miracle of real forgiveness

III

The Choice For Love

Recognizing the hidden influence guilt has in our thinking is necessary to understand why our lives have unfolded the way they have. Accepting we are not victims of the world, we can change our mind to choices that will change our lives is even more significant. Making it clear that the choice is ours, Jesus summarizes our experience in the world this way:

> *"No one can suffer loss unless it be his own decision. No one suffers pain except his choice elects this state for him. No one can grieve nor fear nor think him sick unless these are the outcomes that he wants. And no one dies without his own consent. Nothing occurs but represents your wish, and nothing is omitted that you choose. Here is your world, complete in all details. Here is its whole reality for you."*
>
> W-152.1

Forgiveness and the choice for love begins when the desire to be happy is greater than the need to be right. Being wrong about something triggers our fear that there is something wrong with us. Being right while making someone else wrong assures us that the guilt we have projected onto them is well deserved. While seeing others guilty seems to temporarily avoid the consequences our own guilt would impose, it never makes us happy. Momentarily relieved, perhaps, but never happy. Only when we are able to connect or find a way to join with someone do we feel happy. And forgiveness, by denying that guilt (the cause of our separateness) is real, is the most direct way to bring that about.

We have well disguised the fact that we never judge anyone for what *they* have done, but only for our own hidden feelings of guilt. It is not necessarily even for any specific thing they have done, but simply to keep their guilt fresh in our mind to substitute for our own. Jesus says that to learn forgiveness you cannot overstate the significance of correcting this misunderstanding:

> "Only the self-accused condemn. As you prepare to make a choice that will result in different outcomes, there is first one thing that must be overlearned. It must become a habit of response so typical of everything you do that it becomes your first response to all temptation, and to every situation that occurs. Learn this, and learn it well, for it is here delay of happiness is shortened by a span of time you cannot realize. You never hate your brother for his sins, but only for your own. Whatever form his sins appear to take, it but obscures the fact that you believe them to be yours, and therefore meriting a 'just' attack."
>
> T-31.III.1

Recognizing that we have been responsible for the false self-image we no longer want, it should be obvious *we do not know what to replace it with!* Be very certain you can accept that this is totally true. It must be our clear choice to turn to another Source for knowing, or the new "you" and its supporting thoughts will only parody the old. Nothing will have really changed.

Our desire to be a unique and different self in a world of other different "selves" is bound to collide with their stories of also wanting to be uniquely different. Attack and defense are "normal" in our world. Stress and fear have been familiar feelings. But we are beginning now to realize we do not discover who we are by contrast with one another, but through our oneness with them. Because of our projections, letting go of our judgmental thoughts is best accomplished by wanting to find our brother's innocence along with our own.

It seems we find this union, choice by choice, in what seems to be a process. But what we really do is examine each choice by partially making it, slowly removing the resistance we have to *really* making it completely. Along the way, we examine and decide the value of each piece we must let go. They are actually all the same, yet they all seem different because that is the way we have made this world. So when you run headlong into one that demands to be the exception, you will most likely have the chance to examine it quite often, in many different forms.

The choice between being right or happy becomes more meaningful as you feel the results of choosing love. The happiness you feel when forgiveness is truly offered makes future choices easier. Connecting our happiness to the choice to be loving is the foundation for joining and bringing unconditional peace to our consciousness.

I encourage you not to be discouraged with how challenging this can initially seem to be. One of the primary purposes for our having a network of people doing what we are doing is so that we can see that we are not alone in discovering the inevitable obstacles we will face. We can support one another as we find the inner support that helps us through. Use the network. Share with others what you have found so that you will feel free to ask for help. This is a journey we take together, or not at all.

These choices are not easily made, nor do we initially make them consistently. Our old self-image and the perception that supports it have been our "truth" since time began and is not easily relinquished. But always remember that present in your consciousness is the awareness of another, more loving way to be—along with the means to find it. Be patient with yourself; the results are worth it!

The miracle of real forgiveness

IV

Beyond This World Is A World I Want

There are many teachings that speak of another experience beyond this world; a place where the sorrows, travails and conflicts of this world are unknown. Attainment of this state of mind has been the focus of higher levels of the teaching of Buddhism and other teachings of non-duality, and most recently, in *A Course in Miracles*.

Non-duality refers to the interconnectedness of all things; the singularity of purpose that unifies a single consciousness. Opposites do not exist in a non-dualistic awareness. The most "practical" way for us to learn to over-turn the effects of duality is to begin to see our brother's interests being the same as our own, to see that what we judge him for is a projection of our own guilt. Being free of the need for duality is what most often refer to as the "Awakened" state of mind.

In *A Course In Miracles*, Jesus refers to a "real world." This is not a place of sticks and stones but a state of mind where love surrounds you in the embrace of Oneness and there is nothing to oppose universal happiness and peace. The Holy Spirit holds the Vision of this world and Jesus says there is no one who has not had a glimpse of it, though most seem not to have recognized what they saw.

As someone who has studied *ACIM* for many years, the description of the joyful, peaceful nature of this "other" world has answered an indefinable longing and has encouraged me in my search and practice. I know this longing is in everyone, yet because a world of pure peace and joy is so totally different from what we now experience, it is hard for us to believe it is possible to share this Vision right in the midst of turmoil, especially when we have no first-hand evidence that it exists.

In a recent morning quiet time I was again reading in *ACIM* where Jesus speaks of this. He compares this unstable world of cruel and uncertain values with another world where loss is impossible and love is unopposed. I was reminded that the Holy Spirit holds a Vision of this world for us until we can accept it for ourselves. As often as I had read of this, only then did it finally register: If this Vision is held by the Holy Spirit, which is in our mind, then it is *always* there for us to see.

I would like to share with you what "going there" was like, though words largely fail to express the feeling or the fullness of it. The first thing I became aware of, as I have said, was that this "real world" (this state of mind) *already exists* in our mind now. Until I had begun to accept that the world I now experience is first a state of mind and not a place, seeing there is another world that is also "here" now, would have been very difficult to comprehend. But I have learned that since Mind is the creator of all things, whatever is in our mind is "here" and whatever is accepted as our truth is what our mind "sees" instead of what was perceived as the truth it saw before.

As I took this in, I realized that this other "world" was not just sitting here awaiting some magic moment to replace the one we now see. This was actually the "forgiven" version of the world we have already made, and it will become our "real" world when we have forgiven ourselves and can accept a more loving "place" to be. We are, incidentally, in the process of doing that now. It is already unfolding in our consciousness, even when it sometimes seems the opposite must be true.

What I experienced was such a beautiful lightness and freedom accompanying the feelings and images that began to come into my mind. There was a clear awareness of how obvious it was that what had kept me from seeing this before was *only my belief* that it was something to attain in the future. I am quite sure I have never so fully appreciated how a thought or a belief can so completely skew everything that we see, even selectively hide what doesn't support our current belief!

The feeling of it was that everything I had ever seen before had taken place within a tiny little "box." I recognized my whole world *has been* this little box. It was anything but the huge, limitless thing I had previously thought of as a "universe." It was tiny now, only big enough to show me what being isolated, separate and cut off from the wholeness of Creation is like. I understood then what Jesus has meant when he describes us as now living in a "prison house." What we now think of as past, present and future, even universes and death, are only concepts that conform our experience to what will fit into this "little box" of our own limited beliefs. When mind is free, even the concept of "galaxies" is too limited to contain it.

I wasn't aware if there were or were not beings I could identify; it was more an awareness of recognition rather than physical sight. But I slowly came to realize there is no one "here" I did not know. I would have expected to find those from my past, but somehow there was a bond with everyone. It came to me that my awareness of "knowing" others has been limited by my restricting the awareness of my self to the image of a single being, isolated from others. I then realized this recognition of knowing is all about loving. Being free *means* having no defenses, no reason to withhold love. And I "know" everyone I allow myself to love. With this realization, I was aware that everywhere, without further explanation, *this whole world is "smiling."* That was a knowing far beyond words, a feeling of Oneness I cannot literally describe.

As I wondered about who these "others" were, I knew that for now I needed only accept they are a part of me; the connection to my "whole" Self. Words are failing again. The phrase, "part of me," does not describe what I mean. In the ego's perception that has a different meaning entirely. Words are very inadequate to describe what they were never meant to describe. We have devised them to speak only of the symbols of separateness.

During this experience, as the thought of being a "person" began to fade, it was as if there was nothing left to restrict my mind. I felt the delight and wonder of a child walking into an amusement park with unlimited opportunities for fun and adventure. It wasn't as if there was anything specific to focus on, but it was the indescribable sensation of simply being free! This sense of freedom, I finally realized, was the awareness that there was nothing not a part of me. There were no other thoughts not in harmony with mine, and no thoughts that did not make everyone happy!

I realized then it was only that I had found value in my belief that I had a need to be separate that had been enough to make a "box," a "jail," to imprison my mind. This was at once maddening and laughable.

Understanding the meaning of Oneness from the ego's perspective is very inadequate and distorted. It feels restricting, as though we lose a part of who we are, our "special" uniqueness, by being a part of something else. Yet, the opposite is true. *Only when you are part of everything and everything is part of you, is your mind completely free.* Only then can we begin to think outside our box of isolation. Only here can we begin to understand the nature of what being infinite really means.

I can't really describe all that it was like to feel my mind without the restrictions of my old belief. Free, but in ways I could not have imagined what "free" meant before. There were, for instance, no feelings of being restricted to time or space, though I later learned this "world" still barely clings to "time," since Heaven seems still a step away. But there was no sense that anything begins or ends and no feeling of past or future.

I can better understand now how this world we now see will be transformed when we have changed its purpose. Our present world is an exploration of all the boxes that come from those beliefs in sin, guilt and separation. The "real world" is just the opposite. It is an adventure of the ways we are fulfilled in the freedom that comes with *sharing* choices. It is our natural inclination to find joy in joining and sharing. It is only the thought of something being wrong with us that makes us want to separate, to hide our guilt or project it onto others. When that feeling of wrongness is released, what is revealed is the discovery of what it is like to again find our mind free of that unnatural restriction.

These are some of the feelings I experienced of what it is like to see a different world that is free of the need to be separate. I realize I have had "flashes" of this connected, more "real world" awareness before when I have been focused on the Presence of our God Self. Now that I know "where" it is—that it is being held in our mind for the purpose of our knowing it *now*— makes letting go of this world of mistaken beliefs not only easier, but also a much more desirable thing to do.

f

When we consider letting go of this world to make room in our mind for another more peaceful one, it is inevitable that our thoughts will immediately go to all the things and relationships that we associate with this world and do not want to lose. We do not realize how the thought of separateness distorts *everything* it encompasses, limiting it only to the edges separateness will allow. We do not know there is so much more.

When we think of those we love in this world and feel it is a loss to let them go, we have forgotten it is not *they* we are giving up, but only our misperception of them. Neither they nor we are in a "world", but in a fear-ruled focus of mind. Consider how much greater our love for them will be when we see them free of fear and guilt; how satisfying to know there is no pain for them to suffer and no death to separate us. And where in our one Mind could we go and not be joined with what is part of us?

To find the world where we are free, we must accept the thought of innocent wholeness that allows the Holy Spirit's Vision of the forgiven world to be acceptable. In this way, forgiveness changes the purpose of this world that, in turn, can then bring this more "real," unconditionally loving world into focus.

It is easier now to see how the practice of forgiveness is the opportunity to examine the nooks and crannies where we have hidden our shame and guilt and find the help to let them go. It is the practice of demonstrating how we can change our world one experience at a time, learning we can replace the fear and sadness of our judgments with the joy of loving simply because there is no reason not to!

Changing This World

Our motivation for changing the world determines whether the change will be a help or hindrance for us. If we do it to feel safer or find something we think will make us happy, we will only remodel the world we have made and nothing will have really changed.

To change the world we must change the thoughts, the beliefs that have made it. And to change the beliefs, we must change the image we have of ourselves— the source of all we think is true. Guilt and separation are the components of our belief now and the purpose of this world is to support that belief. Forgiveness is the practice of examining and discarding the judgments that support and reinforce these beliefs. This frees the mind to accept the Presence of the God Self, our "real" Self and a Vision of a more real world to learn and practice thoughts of Oneness.

Of all the limitless choices that the ego's perception holds out to us, in truth there are only two that we can make. We choose either for truth or for illusion; for Oneness or for separation. The choice for separation and all that it entails, is the world we now see. It is the result of every choice the ego makes. For the ego, having no reference in its perception for what Oneness is, cannot choose for truth. But truth remains in our mind in the Presence of the Holy Spirit and we will feel it there when there is nothing we want more.

Forgiveness is the most effective practice for directly reversing the ego's guilty intention and the purpose we have previously had for our thoughts. *But to motivate us to begin the practice, it is necessary that we want what forgiveness offers more than what our judgments bring us.* That is the purpose of the awareness held by our inner Presence, the Vision of our peaceful, loving Self, and the joyful world that arises from it.

Having once felt the freedom and happiness, the harmony and indescribable beauty of this real world, the choice to forgive is more easily made. Although the ego cannot choose for truth, we can choose to remove support from our thoughts of guilt and separateness which open our mind to the Presence that holds truth for us. We can literally choose to accept another Source for our thoughts. The choice for this Source is our acknowledgement that there is an alternative and one that we prefer. Forgiveness now will change our intention toward accepting a loving Self and a world that is the mirror for it.

Forgiveness is the way we become willing to look at all the edges of our "ego box"—the concepts of separation, differences, right and wrong, unworthiness and guilt—and decide to no longer live within those limitations. We realize that there is no loss in giving up these thoughts that make this world. There is no loss in letting go of the image of an unloved and fearful self and accepting what God has given in its place. There is no loss in deciding to be free of our "box" and choose the free and loving world we really want.

There has been a "forgiveness movement" unfolding in our consciousness for some time. We are establishing a Forgiveness Movement web page to bring this more clearly into our awareness. Its function is to support one another in consciously changing the purpose of our experience and our world. It is to look within, knowing this is where we find the great freedom and love of our shared reality. Contrary to everything the world now seems to show us, the real nature of our being is to be loving. And we can use this world for the purpose of rediscovering that awareness; supporting, inspiring and demonstrating the power of loving for one another. This is the goal of real forgiveness and our only real function in the world.

The miracle of really forgiveness

V

One Problem — One Solution

We have made the world with a mind divided against itself. Consequently, it's very nature is comprised of opposites, its conflicts presenting problems numerous and diverse. As quickly as we find answers for them, others come to take their place. "Problem solving" becomes a skill we highly prize.

We are learning that the problems of the world do not originate in the world. They have their beginning in the mistaken beliefs we all fundamentally share and have used to make the world what it seems to be. And while there are many who would like to end the suffering they see in the world, they do not yet know what has really caused it.

There seem to be a wide variety of reasons for things going wrong and many things we need to fix. There are holes in the ozone, global warming, diseases, starvation, racial and cultural hatreds, and personal conflicts at every level. The challenges and struggles vary in form and intensity and are present everywhere. What we do not yet understand is that these challenges and conflicts exist because they are the evidence of *what we expect to find* in a world where everything mirrors our own self-image—where nothing is perfect, whole or complete. They are thoughts in form that confirm our story that something is wrong with us. And the purpose we have given these "thought images" determines the effect they have on us.

The Problem

The one real problem is that we have forgotten what the real problem is. When our mind seemed to split between truth and illusion, it was as though we had separated from our Knowing, lost the awareness of our perfect wholeness, and our connection to all of life. *And now every so-called problem we seem to have portrays the effect of our thinking caused by our belief in separation.*

The loss of the sense of wholeness has also given birth to our idea of "lack." The experience of lack in all its many forms is the manifestation in the world of our belief that we are incomplete. This is also why there are limitations inherent in all our experiences here. Nothing in the world is free of the limitation this belief imposes.

Every kind of problem that seems to exist in the experience of our life in the ego world stems from these beliefs. This is true of "world" problems such as over-population or famine (there won't be enough for everyone); pandemic disease (lack of control of being safe); global warming (lack of resources and lack of control) or prejudice and war (lack of love). It is equally true of what we imagine to be "personal" problems such as lack of money (a lack of self worth); abuse (lack of love) or pain and sickness (lack of innocence).

Because we do identify ourselves as bodies living and satisfying our needs in a world, our belief in lack also shows up as lacking what we need to survive or be fulfilled in that world. *We have forgotten our "natural" Self and so do not identify this forgetfulness as the cause of all lack.*

The world, being the symbol of our belief in separateness, has then mistakenly seemed to be the source of the means to overcome or fulfill the many forms of lack inherent in that belief. We look to better education to get better jobs, and to make more money, thinking that will overcome our lack of self worth. We look to special relationships and make depreciating judgments of others thinking that by comparison we will feel more loved. We punish our bodies with sickness to satisfy our guilt because we think we have lost our innocence and do not deserve to be loved.

Most significantly, we give different identifications and meanings to the different forms of lack, making them seem to be different problems requiring different solutions. Some of the problems we want to change because they bring an obvious discomfort to our lives. Others we do not want to change because they are needed to validate our self-image.

All of the symbols of lack arise from the same source— the belief that we are incomplete—and so they cannot be independently changed but must be addressed at their common source. All are symptoms of the same thought; that we are separate from our innocent and deserving Self, thereby denying the reality, and subsequently, the experience of a whole and complete Self.

The Solution

As all problems we see are symptoms of lack, of feeling separate, *healing any problem then begins with the denial that separateness is real.*

Until we are open to the evaluation of the Holy Spirit as to what the real problem is, we typically pursue solving the problem as we see it and wonder why nothing really changes. The ego will always insist the problem we should be concerned with is what others are doing—with what is happening in the world. To be free to change our world, we must be reminded we are responsible for our experience here. Forgiveness is a process of taking responsibility for how separateness and guilt controls our life, influences every belief we have, and uses our perception as a defense against our *true reality.*

We have most cleverly hidden our own underlying guilt behind beliefs such as right and wrong, what is more or less intelligent or efficient, socially acceptable or morally correct. The list is endless. We have deflected our guilt onto others for whatever reason that best seems to justify our personal story. Then to further distance ourselves from our "sin," we rebel at the thought of accepting—forgiving—this kind of attitude or behavior in others.

Because of this denial, the forgiveness process will inevitably find something, some characteristic someone has, usually someone close to us, which we find nearly impossible to accept. We will strongly resist identifying with it as our own issue. However, we would not have disowned it and attempted to make it "their issue" if we were not threatened by it. So do not be surprised if accepting responsibility for the guilt you see in someone else seems unreasonably hard. It will, more than likely, evoke feelings of sacrifice and injustice because not being the "kind of person" these traits represent has been important in defining our self-image.

Nothing will really change until we take responsibility for what we have projected on to others. It is our own thoughts that make our world, whether we claim them for ourselves, or judge them in others. But until we acknowledge their source, we will have no control over them, and no way to change them.

Accepting Responsibility

To understand the significance of the practice of forgiveness to change our mind, we must also accept it is the power of our mind that has made the world in the first place. It is crucial to recognize that it is only our thoughts and the intention we have for them that is the basis for our experiences and everything that appears to "happen" in the world.

All perception is an accommodation to accept as "true" whatever validates our core belief. And our choice to *want* it to be true is all that is required to make our misperceptions appear to be fact. That is the power of our mind. It is the only real power in all Creation, whether used for illusions or for truth.

In *A Course in Miracles*, Jesus tells us the greatest resistance to forgive is the belief that we are asked to overlook what is real. That is why it is essential to recognize that the belief in sin and separation is contrary to the innocent Oneness of God's Creation, and so cannot be true. When this is realized, the function of forgiveness is understood as correcting a *misperception*, not a fact.

> "The major difficulty that you find in genuine forgiveness on your part is that you still believe you must forgive the truth, and not illusions. You conceive of pardon as a vain attempt to look past what is there, to overlook the truth in an unfounded effort to deceive yourself by making an illusion true. This twisted viewpoint but reflects the hold that the idea of sin retains as yet upon your mind as you regard yourself.
>
> W-134.3

We are not alone in making this great shift from fear and judgment to the freedom of loving as God loves us. From the moment we seemed to succumb to guilt and forgot this joyful feeling, the solution for awakening to our changeless Reality has been available in our mind.

In *A Course In Miracles*, Jesus teaches it is the Holy Spirit that holds the awareness of truth for each of us within our mind, quietly and without judgment, correcting our errors of perception as the means to change our mind and the world that it has made. He tells us that we really have changed nothing but our *awareness* of what is true; that to restore our "right mind" it is only our misperception of the apparent reality of sin that must be undone.

The Split Mind

When we adopted a belief in separation in contradiction of our oneness, our mind became divided between truth and illusion; love and guilt. The part we now primarily assume to be true is attached to the belief in guilt and all the feelings that arise from it such as fear, anger, defense and attack. As a result of the split, our mind now seems to be in a constant state of conflict. It is why every thought that would surrender us to loving is met with feelings that we do not deserve to be loved. This is especially so when we try follow our desire to be peaceful, happy, or loving.

Do not be tempted to underestimate the chasm that exists between what these two very different voices speak of. It is as great as the distinction we would make between Heaven and hell, pure unopposed happiness or inevitable pain and suffering.

Everyone who wants to walk the path of loving inevitably must discover what seems to block their way. It might seem that when we learn it is only our thoughts that deceive us we would rejoice and immediately change them. But this is not the case. We have slowly abdicated the strength of loving to our voice that speaks of fear.

We have countless ways to demonstrate that we must earn the right to play. We are only too familiar with how we expect our happiness to come with a price. Our "shoulds" will always seem to take precedence over what we really want. The demands of guilt have priority because we have accepted that sin, not love, best defines the nature of who we are.

We are afraid that the thought that rises up to tell us something "bad" will happen if we surrender to our innocence, is really true. But this is actually our opportunity to affirm it is the same thought that always opposes our release from fear, *and it has no more effect than we are willing to give it!*

We have become so accustomed to hearing that voice that judges it is easy to think it is the *only* voice to hear. It is helpful to be reminded that our mind does seem split and there is another Voice to hear. This, too, is how forgiveness helps us, illustrating how much better we feel when we don't listen to the ego and choose not to judge.

Knowing there is another choice, we can decide which voice we really want to hear; which one speaks of the outcome that we both want and deserve. It is in choosing if we will listen to the voice that judges or the one that encourages us to forgive that we choose between our own guilt or innocence.

It is knowing this alternative exists that opens our mind to finding it is already there. There still is "work" for us to do, however, for deserving to be loved still seems a challenge. But as practicing forgiveness helps us abandon the thoughts we have used to judge, our more natural urge to join and love will appear. We can then see the Vision of the forgiven world the Holy Spirit holds for us.

VI

The Guide To Real Vision

Our current beliefs are radically different from what we are learning is true. However, there is a Presence in our mind whose sole function is to help us *reinterpret* our perception in such a way that will guide us more easily to a loving and peaceful way to see. This inner Guide is universally present everywhere in our one Mind, acknowledged or not, to focus our learning on the goal of seeing everyone's interest and real desire the same as our own and to remembering our Oneness.

In the New Testament of the Bible, Jesus is quoted as saying:

> *"And I will ask the Father, and He will give you another counselor to be with you forever—the Spirit of Truth. The world cannot accept Him because it neither sees Him nor knows Him. But you know Him, for He lives with you and is in you."*
>
> John14:16

This "counselor," this Spirit of Truth, is what we know as the Holy Spirit. Its purpose is *not* to teach us how to improve or reform our ego self. Nor is it designed to condemn it. But it will teach us how to "purify" our perception by removing the blocks that keep us from recognizing what is true.

A purified perception has discovered there is an alternative to fear and hate. It recognizes there is a more joyful and loving way to live which then welcomes the Vision the Holy Spirit holds. Thus begins the practice of finding our "right mind."

Forgiveness is the practice of letting the Holy Spirit re-evaluate our judgments made from guilt. The peace this brings to our mind is what "purifies" our thoughts, shifting our intention for them to be more in alignment with the nature of our one, whole Self.

Forgiveness left to the ego's interpretation always results in an attempt to make real the "thing" to be forgiven. The ego, for example, would consider it a loving gesture to point out to someone what their faults are, thinking this could then improve their life. This kind of thinking justifies the need to improve our existing perception, maintaining the validity of what it stands for. This is not what forgiveness is finally about and why it is so vital to allow the process to be guided by the Holy Spirit.

The Holy Spirit's Plan

The Holy Spirit has forgiven the world. He has looked into the Mind of God's Son and recognized that his thoughts of terror have no foundation in truth. He knows they are the imagining of a Holy Child who dreams he is not loved. But He knows as well the Father of the Son Who holds us safely in His Mind where the Son was born and will forever live in Love. The Holy Spirit knows the thoughts of both the Father and the Son and is a bridge between these two "worlds."

The Holy Spirit holds this Vision in the place in Mind where the Son seems to sleep, lost in thoughts that block his memory of what is true. It is His purpose to take each thought that would confirm the dream and reinterpret it in such a way that will free him from the belief his fears are real. And this the Holy Spirit does in such a perfect way there is no guilty, fearful thought that It will not return with Love, and so reverse the effect guilt might have had.

The Holy Spirit's plan gives us a way of reinterpreting our thoughts, a way of "seeing" that always results in perfect peace and happiness for everyone equally. The plan unfolds through forgiveness. It assures us that nothing has ever happened in our world, or yet can happen, that does not have a way for it to unfold in perfect harmony with God's plan for our awakening.

In *ACIM* Jesus expresses his encouragement to rely upon our inner Guide by telling us this:

> *"What could you not accept, if you but knew that everything that happens, all events, past, present and to come, are gently planned by One Whose only purpose is your good? Perhaps you have misunderstood His Plan, for He would never offer pain to you. But your defenses did not let you see His loving blessing shine in every step you ever took. While you made plans for death, He led you gently to eternal life."* W-135.18

There has never been a thought anywhere in the ego's consciousness that has not been instantly corrected by the Holy Spirit so that it could be experienced in a helpful and happy way. But our guilt blinds us to this truth the Holy Spirit would show us, and leaves us to experience the effects of our own fearful judgments. To share in the Holy Spirit's Plan we must be willing to accept His Vision of an innocent world, which means we must be willing to accept our own innocence.

This is the function of forgiveness and the only purpose the Holy Spirit sees for the world. As each of us adopts His Plan as our own and uses it to bring peace into our own lives, the more forgiveness, not revenge, is used by others, everywhere, when "solving" the problems of the world.

The Importance Of The Holy Spirit

All of our learning is ultimately dependent upon each of us being able to access an awareness of the truth and use it to develop new habits of thinking. We have this awareness within our mind now, but because it is not part of our familiar perception it can seem to be unreachable. But if we are persistent, our desire to know cannot be denied. Unlikely as it may now appear, in truth, we are at the center of all knowing. It is only our belief in separateness—that minds are individual and independent—that hides this truth from us. Isolation of all things is the effect of our belief in separation. All thought is interconnected; there is no distinction between cause and effect.

In our "unknowing" state of awareness we seem to be the ignorant one who asks to know. Yet it is also we, from our knowing state that answers. The reality of Oneness is our assurance that this is so.

As we access the Holy Spirit's Vision, it will first seem to be separate from our own. But as we learn to use and rely upon it, the gap closes and we will not doubt that it is our vision as well.

I should also clarify that I refer to Holy Spirit, God Self and Real Self interchangeably to identify this Presence. We must remember, however, that whatever words we use, we are always in truth referring to a part of the undifferentiated Oneness.

The Holy Spirit awareness can function as any other awareness we draw upon in our thinking and for the choices we make. The only requirement to claim It is to *want this awareness more than what we have wanted before,* and to want it for everyone—without exception. That means to want to make innocence real instead of guilt; to make love real and not our defenses against love, and to disavow the reality of the world we see by forgiving what we have condemned.

To discover how practical, how "user friendly" the Holy Spirit is, it is helpful for us to dispel the ethereal, abstract concept of what and where the "Presence" of this awareness is. It is experienced as a Thought in our mind, as available to us as any other thought that is not blocked or hidden by another belief we want more.

Listening and following the inner Guide is about far more than what to do in special circumstances. It is learning to consistently, throughout the day, feel the Presence connecting us to every living thing. To begin to feel the familiarity of the harmony and peace that expresses the nature of our Oneness; to experience a state of mind we have nearly forgotten is there.

Whatever It is called, this is the awareness of our Real Self. When we learn to accept the real nature of Its Presence in our mind, we will *know* there is an alternative to our ego perception. The fact that it is present in our mind *now* implies the single most important thing for us to learn—that everything we have always searched for or wished to become, we already have and already are. Every wish to be loved is fulfilled in every instant. We are now whole and complete. It is only our denial of truth that seems to separate us from the acceptance of this eternal gift.

The miracle of real forgiveness

VII

Learning A New Kind Of Forgiveness

Most of us have forgotten that the Grace of God exists eternally within our Mind because the veil of guilt obscures that awareness now. We do not remember that Love is all we felt when we were free of guilt. The meaning of what Oneness is has been lost in a world of differences where everything seems disconnected from everything else.

A Course in Miracles is a teaching of non-duality, an attempt to reawaken our awareness of the Oneness of all Creation. When Jesus was quoted in the Bible as saying such things as, *"My Father and I are One"* and *"The Kingdom of Heaven is within you"*, he was teaching what we now would call "non-duality." He knew there is no opposite to life that we call "death" or that our Spirit cannot be different or separated from the Source that created it. However, in the world of opposites we now perceive, our bodies appear to be born and die with moments of suffering and pleasure in between. These dualistic experiences are not of our Creator's making, but appear as a reflection of our mistaken belief that there is something wrong with us.

There have been other teachings of non-duality, such as

Buddhism and Advaita Vedanta, all working together for the transformation of the ego's need for separation. Yet, there has always been a great resistance to accepting that we are responsible for our experiences. When you believe there is something wrong with you, it is far easier to hold someone else accountable; even to presuming that it is God Who has made the world and is directing our experiences to "redeem" us from our "sins."

The effects of our belief in separateness, pain and suffering, attack and defense, seem to take place in physical bodies in a physical world. These bodies have become the "self" we identify with, and so they seem to suffer the effects of the belief that made them. But in truth, we are pure Spirit remaining untouched and unchanged in any way by any thought not in alignment with our Oneness. Our separate thoughts have impact only in the story we are telling of separateness. As forgiveness frees our mind from how we have judged ourselves, our world, too, is freed and the making of a different world has begun.

To the world's perception of what is real, what *A Course In Miracles* teaches is a radically different way to think and see our world. It will bring peace and joy to our lives and finally help us to discover a truth about ourselves we have forgotten. Its teaching is opposite to all we have previously perceived to be true and so it has taken some time for our "willingness curve" to reach a moment when we could trust enough to consider that what it promises could be true and reachable now.

Jesus summarizes it this way:

"Nothing real can be threatened.
Nothing unreal exists.
Herein lies the peace of God."

There is no one who does not want the kind of peace and lasting joy it speaks of. But we have been so attached to our fearful belief that God made the world as a place to teach us to sacrifice for our sins, there has been no real basis for thinking we *could* change it.

If we want to have a world where peace and happiness are all that we expect, then we must be willing to offer peace and happiness to everyone in the world, for there is no one who is not a part of us. There is nothing we would judge them for and not judge ourselves as well. And if we want this peace and happiness now, then now is when we must be willing to give it. What could happen tomorrow that would make us want it more, or make anyone more deserving to receive it? What could we postpone that would make a happy and a peaceful world more feasible than choosing to have it now?

We, on the other hand, have pursued our healing, our "salvation" from what happened only in a dream, our story of what never could be true. As we begin to realize a vastly different Self exists, the practice of forgiveness will undo our focus on right and wrong and bring us a greater happiness than we can now imagine.

"Salvation is a paradox indeed! What could it be
except a happy dream? It asks you but that you

forgive all things that no one ever did; to overlook what is not there, and not to look upon the unreal as reality. You are but asked to let your will be done, and seek no longer for the things you do not want. And you are asked to let yourself be free of all the dreams of what you never were, and seek no more to substitute the strength of idle wishes for the Will of God."

We are asked to allow our belief to be changed by learning to trust what is real but unseen, and not to judge what is seen in the world, trusting there is nothing "real" in our dreams as we see them. Trusting this more loving way to "see" from the truth of our wholeness is a new kind of forgiveness. It is this process that is needed to redirect our thinking to come from a "place" of Oneness to help us remember what is true and real instead of continuing to make the same old choices that always result in loneliness, pain, and the deception of separation.

Most of us do not know the scope or depth of our belief in "sin" and its need to make us feel separate. We might even say that we don't feel "sinful", and only guilty on occasion. But our guilt is hidden in what we consider normal feelings of anger, loneliness, fear, of something lacking, unworthiness, or the drive to "do" something that we think will make us lovable.

We certainly do not relate to the assertion that guilt controls our normal patterns of thinking. But If it doesn't, what then is the reason for our need to judge right and wrong? Why is there such compulsion to distinguish bad from good? Is this judgment not the basis for nearly every decision we make? And yet, it is our real nature not to judge at all, to instead experience the freedom and the joy of simply "connecting" with one another. If guilt did not distort our thinking, every thought would be a happy one. It is the function of forgiveness to reclaim this peace and freedom.

> *"Forgiveness recognizes what you thought your brother did to you has not occurred. It does not pardon sins and make them real. It sees there was no sin. And in that view are all sins forgiven. What is sin except a false idea about God's Son? Forgiveness merely sees its falsity, and therefore lets it go. What then is free to take its place is now the Will of God."*
>
> WB-II.1.1

On occasions when I have spoken of loving unconditionally, forgiving "unreasonably" because the idea of sin is not true, a very common reaction is that then anyone would feel free to steal, kill, etc., because it wouldn't matter as there would be no consequences. Many believe that without guilt and the fear of punishment there would be nothing to keep us from behaving in the worst manner imaginable.

This is a perfectly logical thought of the ego's perception because it does imagine the worst of itself is true. However, what really is true is quite the opposite! Without our perception of guilt, we can recognize we are as we were created to be: perfectly and absolutely loving. The simple fact is that we all behave in a way that suits the image we have made of ourselves. Can you imagine anyone filled with love doing anything unloving?

Forgiveness is the most direct and effective way we have to get past all our blocks to loving freely.

Forgiveness and Miracles

It is easy to say that forgiveness is learning to see past what really is not there and not judge or value what has no meaning. Easy to say, but hard to do for our unworthy and fearful ego thoughts are the basis for the values which have defined the "self" that we have made. But forgiveness sees no one unworthy of love and frees our mind to experience miracles. A miracle is a glimpse of what the world can be when unencumbered by the distortions guilt and separateness place on it. Forgiveness and miracles are intertwined, each the cause and the effect of the other. Forgiveness opens the mind to move past defenses and the judgments they require. The resulting miracle sees nothing to be forgiven.

Miracles are manifestations of thoughts in the world that contradict the "laws" upon which the world functions. It is because their evidence is so starkly different from the forms our other thoughts take that we say it is a "miracle." The practice of denying the value, the very truth of our thoughts of guilt, is what forgiveness is. It is then accurate to say that miracles are the evidence of forgiveness at work.

The *form* a miracle takes is whatever will most effectively heal your misperception, whatever your "stage" of awareness. It addresses *whatever is needed by each person* in that moment. It will heal sickness if your fear is focused on the body; it will heal relationships if that will best answer what seems needed. Or it can open the door to our Oneness with all Creation if that is what we can accept.

VIII

Our Purpose In The World

---

*"How lovely is the world whose purpose is
forgiveness of God's Son!"*

T-29.VI.6

Remembering our Oneness is the purpose of all our learning. It is the perspective from which our truth will be remembered. We do not now remember what Oneness really is or how it might affect the relationships we value in the world. To learn of it will require that our mind be open and free of the prejudices of the perception we now use to justify our separateness.

In the Workbook of *ACIM*, Jesus describes our true reality:

*"I am one Self, united with my Creator,
At one with every aspect of Creation,
And limitless in power and in peace."*

W-95.11

Despite our belief and all it's appearances to the contrary, even the ego consciousness is undivided. While all the

---

parts seem mainly to be in constant conflict, we are, in fact, functioning as a single entity. The forms of our stories are as different as we can make them, but the outcome of them all is to prove our separateness is real. The "dance" we do with one another is perfect, each perception validating its own version of separation.

Each ego is concerned only with its own version of the story of "what is wrong." But the Holy Spirit sees that all our stories are the same and all are healed in the awareness of our innate and innocent Oneness. It holds a plan for this to happen that directs all our many encounters in such a way that benefits the whole consciousness together, moving it as one toward a single goal.

When we are caught up in the appearance of differences the problems of the world seem overwhelming. There is hate for many different reasons, violence provoked by unrelated causes, pollution of the air we breath and the water we drink, global warming, rape, famine, economic failures, "accidents" of every kind imaginable, individual sickness and mass epidemics, greed, corruption, failed relationships, poverty and . . . well, we are always adding more issues to make sure we don't forget that there is something wrong with us.

The problems of the world seem so pervasive and dominant it would appear to be too overwhelming to try to change them all. Yet when we realize that what we are seeing are *all* the effects of just *one* mistaken belief—sin—it becomes clear there is only *one* thing, *one thought*, we need to change for *all of its effects* to go away.

Hateful, unloving behavior is the inevitable effect of feeling guilty. Sin is only guilt's denial of deserving love. Extending love is what heals the belief we are unloved. The irony is that we will not see or understand this until we have first made the choice to love. Only then is the mind open to recognizing the power of love to heal.

"Teach me how to love," is all we need ask to find our purpose in the world. And forgiveness is the means that will best teach us.

Think on this a moment, for it is absolutely true: *Just past the dream of being separate, there is no one in all the world, no living thing has ever existed, that does not love you.* The great irony and sadness of our story is that the thing we all want most, will go to any length to achieve, we already have.

It is our self-condemnation that leads us to think we live in a dangerous world. But we are all created in Love, from the Presence of Love, and must remain perpetually a part of what Love is. And all that hides our conscious awareness of this is the thought that we have "sinned" and lost the thing that binds us together. Yet, by forgiving what has no meaning, we can remember the unity and peace of our one Self and recapture the Love we seemed to have lost. What better use could we make of our world?

Jesus speaks of the Holy Spirit holding a vision of a "Real World," free of the idea of sin and death, where peace, joy and love are pure and unopposed. It is easy to presume that "someday" this world will surely replace the one we have. But why "someday?" If there is no reason for us not to experience the joy and freedom of our oneness, *why not choose to have it now?* There can be no reason not to have it now that we ourselves have not imposed. And I feel certain that it has been disclosed it to us now because we are ready to accept it now.

The Power of Our Thoughts

One of the chief effects of separateness is the sense of being less than complete or "whole," and separate from what we need to sustain us. We have made a body and a world that seem to be "outside" of us where we can look for what we hope will complete and sustain us instead. But feeling disconnected from the Source of Life, we seem to have no control over our ego life, always thinking things can happen to us.

Not recognizing our Oneness, we try to make a separate, independent self. We have lost the awareness that the power of the one Mind, our real mind, is the only power there is.

Not only do we deny it is our thoughts that make the world, our belief that we are separate is so ingrained we rarely consider the effect our thoughts might have on others. There is a very simple exercise to try that can illustrate we share a single mind.

Pick someone you have a conflict with, someone you tend to avoid because you are uncomfortable in their presence. The next time you have the opportunity to be with them, sit down beforehand and decide if you are ready to love them.

If you feel no resistance affirm that this is what you want. Then ask your God Self to show you how to *let it happen* and watch the outcome unfold. If you have been honest in your desire they will know it and because being loved is a desire we all share, that is what will happen.

If you find resistance to the commitment to love them, ask to see what it is in your mind that would make *you* unlovable. Here you will find what you do not accept about yourself, what wants to be forgiven in you. Now, and this is the only hard part, ask to be shown how to be grateful that they have helped you find what was unacceptable in you. Then ask to be shown how to forgive this "thing" in both of you. Now ask again if you are ready to love them.

Be willing to repeat the process as often as necessary until you find no resistance to loving them or yourself. Be willing to look at every "reason" something in the world *seems more real than your desire to love*; has more value than finding the truth about yourself. This is the purpose of forgiveness and why it is our only function in the world.

A Dialogue with Jesus

In a communication with Jesus, he gave us another illustration of our shared mind and how our thoughts can be used by the Holy Spirit to help one another.

"It is difficult for you to see the impact of your thoughts on others while believing your minds are separate. Yet, your role in seeing a forgiven world is significant for that is what changes the awareness of the ego's consciousness. But please remember it is the Holy Spirit that determines how

your thoughts are used, and frequently in ways you would not recognize. You are still accustomed to using guidance communication on the direct level of receiving a specific answer to a specifically perceived need. It is time for you now to see how the sureness of your loving intention can be used to bring assurance to one in doubt about any issue at all.

"Give no thought to what you may perceive as the distance, cultural or language barriers that may seem prohibitive. You cannot be further from anyone than you are from me at this moment. And it is not your "language" that communicates your intent.

"The magic of separation seems to be complete when you only look outward, but within your mind, there is no distance that separates you from any part of God's Creation. Nor is there distinction made between the many forms of fear to which your loving presence can bring healing.

"I have asked you on occasion to direct your thoughts to circumstances that needed help that you were present to give. I asked you to do this that you might be aware of the impact your thoughts have everywhere, though you were unaware of the circumstances for which they were being used.

"I have said that no intention directed toward the truth is ever wasted. No thought that expresses love ever goes unheard.

"Let me give you a simple explanation of what I mean. You know that every call for help is answered. In a country where perhaps there is hunger, there may be one who feels

hopeless and unable to feed her family. A call is made for help and suddenly a thought of where to find food seems magically to appear in her mind. This may not appear to be related to the loving and freeing thoughts of your forgiveness, but bringing food to a starving family and bringing peace to a mind filled with fear or hatred can equally serve the Holy Spirit's purpose.

"When anyone cries for help, your intention to free the world of pain becomes the means by which that plea is answered. Food for the body and food for the soul comes from the same place.

"There is but one healing that is needed, and that is of your fearful, guilty thoughts. But when a thought cannot seem to move beyond the needs of the body then that is where the first healing must occur. This is why it is so important for you to realize and incorporate in your intention that everyone be healed along with you. You need not know how their needs are best answered, what form their healing will best take, but in your desire to offer healing to everyone, no one can be excluded.

"All problems stem from a perceived lack of love, and so it must be love that heals all problems. It is for you to be the Presence of what healing is, to be the assurance that there are no exclusions to Love. From this awareness, the Holy Spirit is able to cross all the boundaries of ignorance, regardless of its form, and bring your gift where it is needed and in the form it is best understood."

IX

We Walk Together

No matter how it appears, we walk together in this world where we all seem separate. We call no one "enemy" or "friend" who is not, in truth, a part of who we are. No one suffers or is completely free apart from all the rest. Everyone is looking for the truth, but most would not describe what they are after in this way because they are still unaware they are the cause of their world.

Most cannot yet accept that a lack of financial security or a loving relationship is the effect of an unworthy and unloved image of themselves. They would say that what they needed was a better job or relationship. But to help them, and ourselves, we must be able to acknowledge that it is only our acceptance of the truth of our wholeness that will free us from the perception of any need at all.

Everyone wants to be accepted and loved. However, we will never understand this if we focus on, and judge the means they use to find it. There are those whose self-hatred is so severe they think God calls upon them to punish or to kill those who do not believe as they do. To them it is not too great a price to "sacrifice" their life for what they think will earn them God's gratitude and Love.

Then there are those of us whose story is to be a victim and feeling threatened by that choice, our fear calls for a defense against what others do and erects another barrier between us. We cannot yet see that every brother searches for what we also want.

Surrendering our past beliefs is not an easy thing. It will require the use of forgiveness as our daily practice, being diligent to recognize the myriad forms of guilt so subtly present in our thoughts. Then, as we are able, bringing each one to the light of forgiveness. We must learn to listen and to trust that what our guidance is unfolding *for us all* is in perfect time and order.

We can be sure that we share with everyone our desire to find the path to love, simply because we are all a part of the same consciousness that was created *from* Love. When we are not confused about what is true, we know our intention must be the same as theirs, though the form may be radically different. In our truth we cannot want what our brother does not want, nor can we find our way to truth without him. Because we believe that we are separate, we may choose not to see this, but we cannot actually disown what is forever a part of what we are.

Learning To Discern What is True

To give a solid base to forgiving we must learn to tell the difference between what is real and what is false, and then function in our world with that new awareness. *It is* not enough to only understand the difference, we must use our understanding in the choices we make in order for it to become a different belief experience. In *A Course In Miracles,* Jesus explains that we can accept the Holy Spirit's plan even from within a mind that sees itself a victim of the very thing that it has made:

> *"What joins the separated mind and thoughts with Mind and Thought which are forever one? What plan could hold the truth inviolate, yet recognize the need illusions bring, and offer means by which they are undone without attack and with no touch of pain? What but a Thought of God could be this plan, by which the never done is overlooked and sins forgotten which were never real?*
>
> *"Unshaken does the Holy Spirit look on what you see; on sin and pain and death, on grief and separation and on loss. Yet does He know one thing must still be true: God is still Love, and this is not His Will."*
>
> W-99.4 &5

Here we are faced with the ultimate challenge to our belief, our world and all that seems to happen there. What it takes to breech the imagined gap between us is to trust God's Plan in which *". . . the never done is overlooked and sins forgotten which were never real." This is* the direct denial that there is anything true in our perception, anything real in the world that it has made.

It is this assurance the Holy Spirit holds for us that is the basis to forgive. It is our dependence on this awareness that will change our belief and awaken us from our dream, correcting all our misperceptions together because they are all the same. Our mind is changed as we learn to respond to our world with this new Vision, overlooking what is not real. He likens the releasing of our judgments to "salvation," for it frees us from all the effects we had imposed in the name of "sin." And the process of not judging what has no real meaning, he calls "real forgiveness."

To avoid being trapped in the appearances of the world, it is fundamental to know there is no one who does not have the desire—even more—the *need* to love and to be loved. This comes from a knowing in the deepest part of our being that loving is natural and necessary to be happy and free to live beyond the limits of fear. The desire to love is the foundation of our Being and it will blossom into our awareness as we release the judgments we use to separate us, as we release our resistance to giving love freely, everywhere.

An Attack Or A Call For Love?

A key element in our learning to discern what is true and exercise real forgiveness is our ability to correctly understand what motivates the ego perception. Because it sees *everything* as an extension of its own guilt, its actions can be described as either attacking another's guilt or defending itself from what it perceives as its own guilt. This is true from the most overt situations such as war, or in the more subtle ways it decides who is worthy to love.

The ego's perception is made to prove we are different from everyone else. *This is needed to separate us from the ones on whom we have projected our guilt.* Learning that we walk together here, each of us wanting *exactly* the same thing, is fundamental to finding peace and the truth of our Oneness. But to see who walks with you, first you must recognize that your fears and desires are the same as theirs. Forgiving the judgments that have made these appearances real and hidden this from us is essential to recognize that what we have formerly seen as attack is better understood as a call for love.

What does our brother or our sister really want of us? It's easy to be deceived. But no matter how it looks, it is exactly what we want of them. We have tried to project our self-guilt onto them to make them "worse" than we. And they have done the same. Both of us have tried to rid ourselves of our shame and hate, for with it we did not believe we could be loved. We have attacked one another as "proof" of their guilt, hoping that would hide what we thought was true about us.

Because guilt is the foundation of the ego's perception, attack and defense is "natural" to the way we think and act. And the outcome of every attack or defense will seem justified, its outcome a mirror of our intent. But if we are to learn to forgive and see beyond what our perception thinks is true, we must recognize that the purpose for our attack was motivated by our need to be loved.

But what is there to judge or fear from one who looks to you for love? When you think that he attacks, your defense will separate you; think he looks for love and you will gladly find love within yourself to give and join with him. This is the interpretation the Holy Spirit always offers us. It is necessary we see this if we are to find a world that is free of attack. Think how you would like to feel toward a best friend, the one you would never accuse and always trust completely. Without the defenses raised by self- judgment, this is how you would feel toward everyone. You do not mistrust or hate your brother for what he is, but what you secretly believe you are. What he does now is what you expect of him. The meaning you give to what you see him do is how you evaluate yourself.

Recognize that what seems to be your brother's attack on you is not about you, but is a projection of his judgment of himself. This makes it much easier to understand that what he really wants is to be free of his own condemnation. His projection onto you of his attack upon himself makes this apparent. This is what you give him when you refuse to see attack and answer him with acceptance and compassion. And in the recognition of his innocence you have acknowledged your own and freed yourself as well.

What our brother wants of us and we of him is the same. We are alike, different only in the form in which our belief appears. Our long history of attack and defense and the walls they have built between us cannot change what is true. But until we have changed the pattern of our thinking, it will continue as before. When we see that what they want and what we want beneath the guise of attack are just the same, both of us are forgiven together.

If you hesitate, fearful that your lack of defenses would make you vulnerable to another's attack, it is because you have not forgiven yourself and see your own attack on them still needed to hide what you think is wrong with you.

This is a monumental change to make. Initially, its only justification seems to come through personally experiencing the "miracles" of peace and acceptance that happens when we do forgive.

Everyone wants the same thing: to know that they are loved, and capable of loving. This cannot be overemphasized. It is paramount to exercising forgiveness. No matter how it looks or what the circumstances seem to be, we walk the same path in a world made to make everything look different. Who is "brother" or who is "terrorist" depends *only* on whether you decide they walk with you or they have a different purpose.

Look for guilt and you will find attack. See attack and you will defend. Forgive and see a call for love and you will recognize what it is you want and offer them the same. Be free of judging your brother or his motives, and you will find your own innocence reflected everywhere. We walk together and are free, or walk apart and lose ourselves in the gap that guilt has used to separate us.

The miracle of real forgiveness

X

Forgiveness Is A Function We Can Share

"Forgiveness is the only function meaningful in time. Forgiveness is for all. But when it rests on all it is complete, and every function of this world completed with it. Then is time no more. Yet while in time, there is still much to do. And each must do what is allotted him, for on his part does all the plan depend.

T-25.VI.5

As part of a dialogue I had with Jesus several years ago, he said,

"Your function is to see the face of Christ now hidden in the shadows of the world of time. When you are tempted to judge what he does there, ask the Holy Spirit to show you how to see him as He does. You will see him then bathed in a light that brings joy to your heart, not judgment, and you will see that you stand there with him. The only shadow that can hide the truth of your brother is in your denial of the light that is in you.

"This is the lesson of forgiveness. Learn it well, for you have here discovered it is your vision that will

change your world. Join with me that together we
may be witness to this gift of Vision that has been
given us to share."

He has also said that joining in such a common purpose is for the ego perception as close an intention for experiencing union of which it is capable. This establishes a state of mind that is more accepting of the Holy Spirit's Vision of our brother and our forgiven world.

We have mistaken the world we have made for God's Creation. This makes it easy to assume God also created our bodies and that what they do plays some role in who we are. It is hard to remember that neither our body nor what its eyes see has anything to do with what is true and is never justification for condemning. Jesus reminds us of the innate love we have for one another that is hidden by our guilty judgments:

"Can you imagine how beautiful those you forgive
will look to you? In no fantasy have you ever seen
anything so lovely. Nothing you see here, sleeping
or waking, comes near to such loveliness. And
nothing will you value like unto this, nor hold so
dear. Nothing that you remember that made your
heart sing with joy has ever brought you even a
little part of the happiness this sight will bring you.
For you will see the Son of God. You will behold the
beauty the Holy Spirit loves to look upon, and which
He thanks the Father for. He was created to see this
for you, until you learned to see it for yourself. And
all His teaching leads to seeing it and giving thanks
with Him."

T-17.II.1

65

Understanding the greater power and value of making forgiveness our *shared* function, we can use the Forgiveness Movement (see chapter XXII: *Joining Hands and Hearts*) to better support our *common* purpose. Sharing your success helps strengthen the resolve in someone who seems to have faltered. And when things are not going well for you, their positive experience can renew your own determination. We should also keep in mind this is the movement of our *entire* consciousness toward the truth, regardless of any appearances to the contrary, including those who may appear to be headed in the opposite direction. The Holy Spirit sees no one who is not a part of this movement.

The Function of Real Forgiveness

Real forgiveness is an attitude of non-judgment, justified because the things and people we judge are false images our fearful, guilty thoughts have made. These untrue thoughts have made our world and so the experience of what happens there has no *real* meaning and no effect on what is true. Real forgiveness finds nothing to judge, allowing a vision of innocent Oneness to replace the ego's perception of all the world stands for.

However, *this awareness* has no meaning to the vast majority of people in our world, struggling to simply "survive" the rigors of the world we have made. Taking responsibility for their hunger and their misery, forgiving the one who seems to persecute them because the world is not real and they are not a body will not seem helpful to them until they are moved to seek for answers beyond their perception.

That being said, it is also true that our consciousness now has been opened to this awareness that is leading us all to find the truth. Change is occurring at every "level" of our awareness. What is required to reach each of these levels of self-denial, and the form that will most effectively achieve it, is something beyond our ability to comprehend, let alone try to achieve. That is the function of the Holy Spirit, the reason and purpose He exists in our one Mind. But it *is* for us to know our part and trust there are others at every level who are doing the same—both consciously and unconsciously—that will hasten a broader acceptance of the truth.

It is easy for us to be discouraged when we think we must be in charge of this happening and cannot figure out how to do it. It is also tempting to want to "educate" everyone else, thinking what they need to learn is what we have learned, in the way we have learned it. The more quickly we get past that the more peaceful our own journey will be.

Our surrender of guilt and its fearful ideas will come in many forms and frequently from unexpected places. Many will not be recognized for what they are. But all will contribute to "undoing" our need to make others wrong in order to hide our own guilt. There will be many reasons we find to work together that will eventually remind us of our Oneness. Many will be orchestrated in ways we may not recognize, but all will be healing our fears in whatever form and at whatever level they exist.

But there is something we can do that will satisfy our need to help and also *be* a real help. We can recognize the one thing we all do have in common in our story of the world. We can recognize our own desire to be loved and our need to know we are capable of loving. We can remember as we forgive there is this one intention that reaches through all the levels of understanding and opens every mind to find an alternative to self-hate and to begin their journey to the light.

The world is changing. Our *recognition* that this is so will bring it about even more quickly, for the awareness we each bring to the consciousness *is* the awakening process. This is a journey we must take together. It is not possible for one to be left behind, for no one can be separated from the rest. There is no one in whom God is less present than in any other one.

f

There will never be a better time to change our mind. There is nothing more we need to learn. We need merely to accept what we *have* learned and welcome the Presence of the Teacher within that God has given us to make attainment of our purpose here a certainty. We do not need to wait until the world seems more ready to join us in our story. We are the world and our stories are all the same.

There is nothing that is not a part of us, no one who will not respond to our honest desire to love them. Our choice to have a better world for everyone is a choice that must, and will, be shared by all, when there is no resistance to our being forgiven.

The purpose of our learning is to remember our Oneness. Truly accepting that everyone wants the same thing, no matter what they may misperceive as necessary to achieve it, makes forgiveness easier. Recognizing that there is nothing happening in our world that does not move us toward our common goal strengthens our trust that the Holy Spirit's Vision will be realized.

When truly understood and accepted, these principles make it possible for us to feel a unity of purpose we have not known before. When we finally know no one in truth opposes us with a different goal, then we will have given real meaning to what "unity" is. Thus is the foundation laid in our consciousness for a peaceful and harmonious world.

The miracle of real forgiveness

XI

Idle Wishes And Grievances

Choosing to let go of pain, a grievance, or any other expression of guilt that has seemed to give our life meaning and define who we are inevitably results in feeling better. This is because while we seem to forgive others, *it is always ourselves that we first set free.* A mind free of the need to judge has had the greatest of all burdens lifted from it.

Despite how "righteous" it may appear to condemn a perceived wrong, truly surrendering our judgments will release us to love and to the far greater joy that love brings. But this intention must be given to the One Who knows how to make it work. Which of us has not experienced, while basking in our own good intentions, "something" that comes along and seems to drag us back into anger and judgment? Everyone has felt this because the roots of our guilt go to the very foundation of our self-image and how we see the world. Without the perspective and help of our Holy Spirit, our most "insignificant" ego thoughts will in some way remind us of something fearful in our past and revive the urge to judge ourselves.

What guilt first makes real will not be easily forgiven. We have accumulated countless grievances through lifetimes of judgment and accusation. When seen correctly, they are a clear indication of our need to judge others only as a substitute for condemning ourselves. Think for a moment of those times you have lost your peace just when things seemed to be going well. You will quickly recognize it was the resurrection of some old grievance, buried perhaps, but rising again with seemingly no conscious provocation. We cannot yet acknowledge that the images in the world we made were intended to take the blame for what we believed we were guilty of. So even our most "innocent" interaction with our own feelings of guilt will naturally find a way to remind us of the reason they are there.

> "Idle wishes and grievances are partners or co-makers in picturing the world you see. The wishes of the ego gave rise to it, and the ego's need for grievances, which are necessary to maintain it, peoples it with figures that seem to attack you and call for 'righteous' judgment. These figures become the middlemen the ego employs to traffic in grievances. They stand between your awareness and your brother's reality. Beholding them, you do not know your brothers or your Self."
>
> WB73:2

Misperceived guilt is like a murky pot from which our thoughts arise, and what each thought expresses is tainted by it. If we think of something we like to do, guilt will insist there is something else that should take precedence. We are all familiar with feelings of happiness being followed by the expectation that something most likely will then "go wrong." We rarely allow ourselves to love without defenses, believing there must be a need to guard against rejection. These are only a few of the examples of how guilt slants the intention of our thoughts, while yet allowing enough pleasure to maintain our attachment to the world we now see so that we are less tempted to find a better way.

Forgiveness frees us to use the world to find those hidden places in our belief where we still harbor guilt. It changes the purpose of the world from one of confusion and uncertainty, vengeance and attack, to one of being a positive force in our awakening.

The miracle of real forgiveness

XII

Freedom From Attack

The only way to be completely immune to attack of any kind is to become defenseless. Being defenseless means we have removed the *purpose* for attack from our thoughts so there is nothing in our mind to bring attack into our experience of this world. This makes no sense to the belief that we are separate and independent from one another, and that the world is independent of our thoughts. Yet, correspondingly, once we begin to see how all our "scripts" are interwoven, each one "supporting" the others it is involved with, *nothing else does make sense.*

Defenses strengthen what they defend against. They cannot make you safe for your need for them assures that you will be attacked. Understanding that we make the world by projecting our guilty thoughts outward, we can see how all defenses are a form of self attack. They do nothing to prevent attack, but are actually an invitation to be attacked.

The Blame Game

The fine art of projection is what has made the world all it seems to be. It is the "safe house" where we keep our guilt concealed and secure, assigned to the care and custody of our brothers. Judging them, it remains hidden from our "external" sight but, in fact, it is never far away. No matter how hard we try to be rid of it, its effects are always close at hand. It is the cause of all our fear and anger, sense of lack, failed relationships, insecurities and pain and sickness of every kind.

There would be no purpose for the ego's version of the world if it had no need to project its guilt. The ego's world is a two-way mirror. It exactly reflects from the inside -out all of its beliefs of what it perceives is wrong with it. Then it sees these beliefs from the other side—the outside—as though its sins belonged to the world and it now suffers those effects. Seeing like this, it then believes it is the victim of what it sees, not realizing it is only its own belief. It still suffers the payment guilt demands, but at what seems to be the hand of an avenging world.

The world you see is but an expanded and projected image of yourself, thinking your thoughts, yet seeming to insulate you from their effects. Don't be surprised at all the "obvious" ways you can think of to deny this can be true. You will find yourself saying, "I am not a terrorist, I have no wish to kill and maim; I would never abuse a child, flagrantly steal from others or participate in genocide."

In truth, *no one* would do those things. Even the ones we have accused of these "crimes" would not describe or define them as we have. To the one we call a "terrorist," killing can seem to serve a "holy" purpose. Yet the net effect of the fear and anger we feel in our judgment of *them* matches the self-condemnation our own guilt has imposed on *us*. But making their crimes "worse" ensures they will always bear the brunt of blame because the purpose of it all is to make sure our guilt will seem to rest on *them*.

Each of us must ultimately question what we value most, the "blame game," or the possibility of being free of the "gifts" that the blame and guilt have brought us. If we choose to be free, then it is necessary we understand that it is our own guilt that keeps us prisoner. As we forgive all the appearances of the world, we will discover they can be changed because it is our thoughts that have made them. We can look upon each thing to be forgiven and assure ourselves, "This is of my own doing and it is this I choose to change."

The decision to value love more than the defense against love appeals to an instinct now only dimly remembered. But it is the reawakening of this memory that leads us to the Presence of our God Self and activates the loving Vision held for us there. Then, from that place, it is easily apparent that what we forgive is only the fantasy of our fearful dreams.

Closing the gap between what we now believe and the experience of this new awareness is a miracle and this is exactly where the practice of real forgiveness takes us. It changes our belief that sin is real and replaces the image of an enemy with a brother looking to be loved. It changes the character and purpose of the world. It is indeed a miracle.

"What I (now) see is a form of vengeance. The world
I see is hardly the representation of loving thoughts.

It is a picture of attack on everything by everything.
It is anything but a reflection of the love of God and
the love of his Son. It is my own attack thoughts
that give rise to this picture. My loving thoughts
will save me from this perception of the world, and
give me the peace God intended me to have.

"Without attack thoughts, I could not see a world
of attack. As forgiveness allows love to return to my
awareness, I will see a world of peace and safety and
joy. And it is this I choose to see, in place of what I
look on now."

W-55.2&3

No one attacks another if they are at peace within themselves. Everything we "see" externally, in the world, is a
mirror for the inner image we have of ourselves. Everything.
It is a world made of thoughts and so it must reflect the
mind of the thinker. By this principle then, no one will be
attacked by another if they are at peace with themselves.
No matter how it appears, we are all joined within a single
mind and consciousness, each of us responding perfectly
to one another's beliefs. Those who would be attacked will
find the one for whom being the "aggressor" best suits their
story.

Regardless of how hard we try to make it otherwise, this
is a "mental" world. We are not upset by what someone
does, but by our interpretation of what that means to our
self-image. All attack and defense directed outward are
symptoms of our own inner conflict. That is why war can
never win a peace. It never addresses or satisfies the real
cause of the conflict, which is within the self-perception of
both the one who attacks and the one who seems a victim of

the attack. The only sure result of conflict is that the cycle of attack and defense will go on and on.

These are hard words to hear, particularly when there are children that seem to bear the brunt of the suffering. It is hard to imagine that anyone, let alone a child, would find anything of value in the many kinds of terrible pain we have witnessed in our world. But the truth remains, our experience in this world can only be a story made from the script of our beliefs. What seems a child this time around is carrying the baggage of many lifetimes of stories and they will continue in one form or another until the belief is changed. More importantly, what is also true is that there is no story strong enough to change the nature of our infinite and loving Self. There is no death. There is no pain that can or will survive our story. One day all the stories will end. And when they do, nothing will remain that interferes with our Vision of God's Perfect Son.

As hard as it may be to accept that we are responsible for our life experiences, this is really the "good news" side of the story. It means that it is we who can change our world from one of pain to one of peace. Forgiveness breaks the cycle of attack and revenge by acknowledging that no one has done anything to us. We are free to love them, and so to find our own loving Self. Whether you are able to see the world as an illusion, or simply that you are responsible for your own story in it, you will have found no justification to condemn anyone for playing the part you asked of them. Nor will you long have reason to play the part you accepted for yourself. With this awareness, we can understand what it means to be free in this world.

The miracle of real forgiveness

XIII

Forgiveness And Healing Sickness

As has been stressed, sin and separation are the foundation of our belief and our experience in the world. Sickness is the most explicit illustration that this is true. When we are sick there seems little question there is something wrong with us, and it most effectively satisfies our desire to further withdraw or separate from everyone. And who would want to *really* join with someone whose sickness was a threat to what they most feared would happen to them?

Sickness is not *first* a physical condition. It finds a home in the body because that is where we think we live. We have made the body to fulfill the expectations of being a guilty person; as weak and limited, the instrument of atonement for our sins. This is the inner image we have of who we think we are. The body is simply the physical manifestation of this image of separateness. Pain and sickness in the body satisfies mind's need to atone for its guilt.

The cause of sickness is not in the body. It is the thought of guilt in our mind. Healing sickness therefore is not about healing the body, but removing from the mind the thought that made sickness possible.

Reversing the belief in sickness can most directly be summarized in this way:

- Sickness is only possible where there is guilt.
- Guilt comes from sin which is not possible in God's Creation, and so must be an illusion everywhere.
- I cannot be sick because I have not sinned.

Jesus explains it like this:

"Atonement (acceptance of our innocence) *heals with certainty, and cures all sickness. For the mind which understands that sickness can be nothing but a dream is not deceived by forms the dream may take."*

W.140-4.1

It will seem foolish in the ego's perception of being a body living in a world, to say, "I cannot be sick" when pain is such a dominant force in its experience. But what we are doing here is changing our mind by learning to accept what is true to replace the ego's perception that is not true. And the truth is, that when we have accepted that we are the thought of God and not the thought of sin, there will be no sickness.

We are not the body that houses our dreams. Our Oneness guarantees we are the Presence of what God Is. This is the perspective from which we must learn to see if we are to open our mind to the truth.

Forgiveness is the process of helping us find the places in our mind where sin and sickness still hide. Aside from the mind's healing, the body needs no healing of its own for it portrays only a physical image of what the mind believes is true about itself. It neither does nor feels anything of its own accord. In truth, without the mind's need for the body, it does not exist at all.

We have no real concept of the power of our mind to create or to heal because we use it now to make-up ego stories of lack and suffering. We use it to "disconnect" from the majesty of what was created whole and complete. We think it is separate from all it has made and have only the memory of using it to serve the ego's fearful purposes. We think of it as frail, limited, and undependable because that has been our experience of the effects we expect from the ego's guilty thinking. Learning to use it for a different purpose requires that we begin to think outside the box guilt has imposed; to assume that the "best" and not the worst is true.

The Mind-Body Connection

Recently there has been much made of the importance of recognizing the "mind-body connection." Learning to "listen" to the body is thought to be important to know the body's needs. This would be true if the body had some way of communicating with us and if, in fact, it had needs of its own. But there is no consciousness in the body, no memory and no way for it to communicate with the mind. The only needs it has are those assigned to it by the mind. Feelings that seem to come from the body do not exist until they are registered by the mind. This has been frequently illustrated through the use of hypnosis.

It is because we think of ourselves as a mind-body combination that the body suffers the consequences of minds misperceptions of weakness and lack and all the needs that go along with thinking that we are incomplete. In this thinking, the list of the body's needs is endless: from food to exercise, oxygen to temperature control. It must be protected from the environment and disease and the attack of other bodies. However, aside from what mind assigns to it, the body has no needs at all.

We accept sickness and death because that is the expectation of guilt. We are, however, in the process of changing that belief and coming to recognize there is another way to see ourselves and another, more peaceful and loving world to experience—one without pain and suffering. There is also no need for us to think sickness is "normal" while we are changing our mind. Part of our learning curve of the true nature of our infinite Self is to accept that the body plays no part in who we are. To have a healthy body while guilt is still present in our mind, requires that we see the body "disconnected" from the image of the self we see. It would not then take on the role of bearing the brunt of the ego's guilt.

Relinquishing the body as part of our self-identification is an integral part of learning that the world we now see is not real, that it is the symbol of our separateness. It also releases the body from needlessly experiencing the effects of our misperceived beliefs. This is the only "defense" the body needs to be free of sickness. All of the other things we do to protect the body merely reinforce our attachment to it and assure us that it will suffer the effects of our belief that there is something wrong with us.

How simple that sounds, but what could be more of a challenge to our belief? How many of us can now even begin to relate to who we are without our body? But this is where we must go in our thinking if we are to open our mind to find the truth of who we are. Here too the use of forgiveness is our most valuable tool.

As we begin our learning, simply thinking we must let the body go because it has nothing to do with who we are, is going to be more an intellectual exercise than a serious idea. It is like considering giving up this world while we still think we get something from it. There seems to be too much sacrifice for us to really want to do this. However, in this world, the body can still serve a useful purpose; it can be the means we use to communicate with other bodies. But just to say this is now the function we will use it for doesn't mean our attachment to it as part of our self is finished. That requires some work. It is the same work we have been doing, but with a greater clarity of purpose.

Forgiving and changing our mind is not about having a better body, one that will never be sick or feel pain. But it serves no purpose at all for us to be sick or have pain while we are making the transition from guilt to innocence in our thinking. The trick, as always, is to stay clear about our intention; to stay in the Presence of our real, unconflicted Self and the movement to Truth that is there.

While believing that our mind and our body are connected—partners in who we are—whatever upset is in our mind will show up in our body. There are primarily three things we can do to change our mind about having a need for that partnership:

1. Give the body a different purpose, rather than struggling with the "need" to discard it. Accepting it as the means to interact with other bodies and communicate forgiveness in a loving way gives it a valuable and useful function.

2. As part of the forgiveness process, pay particular attention to the judgments you make of other bodies. Notice how you confuse their behavior and the way their body looks with who they are, influencing the ease with which you accept or reject them. Pay attention to how much you value them for what they do. These are reminders of the choices we are making to distinguish between what is real and what is not. Each time we are able to see the face of love without a body attached to it, we have freed ourselves a little more from what the body symbolizes and opened our mind to Oneness. And we have also lessened our attachment to our own body as a place to experience our misperceptions.

3. The most common way we have of proving our unworthiness is to give our body a purpose it cannot fulfill. For example, thinking our happiness is outside us, in the world, we ask our body to do something there that we hope will make us happy. The problem is, there is no happiness (or despair) in the *doing* of anything but the body, then seeming to be the cause of the failure of the "doing," will

suffer the abuse of failure. Think of all the occasions when you expect to do something that will make you happy. Then remember there is *nothing* that will make you happy outside of your mind's basic *choice to be happy.* Release your body from the expectation to perform functions it cannot do.

These are the practices, as part of our forgiveness process, that will change our mind about the function and the purpose of a body, providing a perfectly functioning mechanism to teach and communicate forgiveness in the world.

It will, for a while, be tempting to use the body's health as a barometer for our spiritual "progress." The ego will quickly seize the opportunity to use any sickness or accident to further its cause of guilt. The truth is that while we are transitioning through the "evolution" of the forgiveness process, surrendering ever more deeply the guilty thoughts we value most, there will likely be sickness. It is helpful, especially now, to forgive these thoughts so that guilt cannot find yet a deeper place to hide.

Real forgiveness will heal our mind of the need for sickness and ultimately will put an end to death, but this is not its real purpose. If correctly understood, it heals our mind of the one thing that now distorts our awareness, creates a universe of pain and hides the truth from us:

> *"Forgiveness is the only function here, and serves to bring the joy this world denies to every aspect of God's Son where sin was thought to rule. Perhaps*

you do not see the role forgiveness plays in ending death and all beliefs that rise from mists of guilt. Sins are beliefs that you impose between your brother and yourself. They limit you to time and place, and give a little space to you, another little space to him. This separating off is symbolized, in your perception, by a body which is clearly separate and a thing apart. Yet what this symbol represents is but your wish to be apart and separate.

"Forgiveness takes away what stands between your brother and yourself. It is the wish that you be joined with him, and not apart. We call it 'wish' because it still conceives of other choices, and has not yet reached beyond the world of choice entirely. Yet is this wish in line with Heaven's state, and not in opposition to God's Will."

T-26.VII.8.5

This is real forgiveness as the Holy Spirit sees it. This is the awareness that heals. And by forgiving what has no meaning in our world, this is the awareness we make real in our consciousness, opening the door to a peaceful world as well as a healed body.

The miracle of real forgiveness

XIV
The Holy Spirit's Vision Of A "Real World"

"The real world is the state of mind in which the only purpose of the world is seen to be forgiveness. Fear is not its goal, for the escape from guilt becomes its aim. The value of forgiveness is perceived and takes the place of idols, which are sought no longer, for their 'gifts' are not held dear. No rules are idly set, and no demands are made of anyone or anything to twist and fit into the dream of fear. Instead, there is a wish to understand all things created as they really are. And it is recognized that all things must be forgiven, before they can be understood."

T-30.V.1

It is difficult to finally begin to see that this world holds nothing of value, has nothing that we want, and then consider there is another world, one that *is* very helpful to us. Introducing the idea of another world can be confusing when we are just trying to imagine what it would be like to let this one go. But there is a distinct reason and much to be gained from learning why this Vision is now held in Mind for us to see.

We are never asked to do something that would invoke a feeling of sacrifice. And while there is nothing of value in this world, we are attached to it. But we are not asked to let it go with nothing to replace it. This would only raise additional resistance and make the ultimate surrendering of our ego goals more difficult. The purpose of being able to share the Vision of the "real world" is to help ease us over this "bump" of resistance.

Our present world is made from thoughts that deny our Oneness. There is nowhere for it to go except into different versions of separateness, and so it goes nowhere. The "real world" is a state of mind where all its parts function in harmony as one. There is no guilt to project that would drive our brother away, but an intention to love that draws him to us. It is the awareness that points us toward accepting the reality of what Oneness actually is.

The most direct way for us to deny our allegiance to separation is to refuse to live as though guilt is real.

Forgiveness is the practice of replacing the goals of sin and guilt in our consciousness with a desire to find a common purpose to pursue. The more we practice, the easier it will become to recognize there is no justification for condemning a dream that has no meaning. And as our guilt diminishes, so will our world be freed from what the thoughts of guilt have made. Without a need for guilt, pain and fear, hate and even "death" will serve no purpose and so will be gone.

The real world will not just "happen" to us any more than this one does. The Holy Spirit is reinterpreting our thoughts, showing us that without the need for guilt there is a way of thinking that will bring peace, and we can find a different purpose for this world to serve. It will then become the opportunity to heal our need for sickness and for war. It will instead fulfill our desire to love again.

Wanting only a world that love has made is important to the journey taken here. It reminds us that "letting love in" is a choice we always have. And when we understand it is our brother's deepest wish as well, what had seemed before to be his resistance and opposition need no longer be an obstacle to finding our common ground.

We do not now understand how this could come to pass because we still imagine there are many separate minds. But in our choice to forgive, the thoughts that have made us seem separate are overturned and we are freed to accept our heart's real desire: to join our brother in peace. Here we have given the Holy Spirit a willingness to see our brother's interest the same as ours. We can see that his desire now resonates with our own. Our mind is now receptive to be taught the only lessons necessary for us to learn:

> "The lessons to be learned are only two. Each has its outcome in a different world. And each world follows surely from its source. The certain outcome of the lesson that God's Son is guilty is the world you see. It is a world of terror and despair. Nor is there hope of happiness in it. There is no joy that you can seek for here and hope to find. Yet this is not the only outcome which your learning can produce. However much you may have over-learned your chosen task, the lesson that reflects the Love of God is stronger still. And you will learn God's Son is

innocent, and see another world. The outcome of the lesson that God's Son is guiltless is a world in which there is no fear, and everything is lit with hope and sparkles with a gentle friendliness. Nothing but calls to you in soft appeal to be your friend, and let it join with you. And never does a call remain unheard, misunderstood, nor left unanswered in the selfsame tongue in which the call was made. And you will understand it was this call that everyone and everything within the world has always made, but you have not perceived it as it was. And now you see you were mistaken. You had been deceived by forms the call was hidden in. And so you did not hear it, and had lost a friend who always wanted to be part of you. The soft eternal calling of each part of God's Creation to the whole is heard throughout the world this second lesson brings."

T-31.I.7&8

There is no one who does not want to be happy and at peace, no one who does not want to be loved. Yet, the world we now see seems to be becoming progressively more chaotic. There are the problems of economic crisis, famine, war and disease epidemics running rampant. Each day something new is added to the mix. These are the thought forms that are expressing our confusion and doubt, as we decide to abandon our defenses against each other, and consider the possibility of our Oneness.

In our split mind, there is a part of us that wants to move ahead, and a part that still listens to its fearful voice. We have long looked to our defenses for safety, but as proven by our history, that has never worked. Yet, the thought of setting them aside is a scary one and so, before we do it, we are bringing up all the reasons those defenses still seem to be needed.

Following the guidance of the Holy Spirit, our forgiveness becomes the means for laying the foundation for His "real world" in our consciousness. It is not a world our ego thoughts can make, nor is it one we will resist much longer. As we accept His Plan for real forgiveness, our purpose is joined with His and we can confidently see how surely our goal will now be reached. The rest of the way we can go in peace, for now at last we can see our journey's end.

The miracle of real forgiveness

XV

An Attitude Of Oneness

Our learning that we have made the world and that we can change our experience here evolves through progressive levels of understanding. We begin by learning that the world is really a state of mind reflecting a belief we have previously referred to as "sin and separation." This is the foundation of the "universal" belief held by our one consciousness. Because that universal belief is being expressed from the point of view of separateness and differences, what then seems to be the different and disconnected parts also seem to have different and disconnected stories. We can now begin to realize they all are actually the same, illustrating only the many ways sin and separation can be experienced.

It is natural that as we learn it is we who have made our painful story and that we can change it, we will try to change it in the context that we have made it true. In other words, if our personal story has centered on sickness, lack, persecution, sacrifice or any of the other myriad ways we make sin and guilt real, these *symptoms* will seem to be the cause of our fear and pain and so they will become the focus of what we feel a need to heal.

What we do not see is that we have predetermined the outcome of *all* our stories within the "universal" story that there is something wrong with us. We do not see that all the stories are the same, only variations on the theme of separateness. Learning we can change our individual stories has been necessary. It has breached the belief that the world happens to us and awakened us to the possibility that something else does exist beyond the edge of our perception. But the stories will continue until we have abandoned the central belief that we are separate.

Forgiveness has opened our consciousness to the real alternative of loving. But the possibility of confusion and misunderstanding still exists. Many of us work very hard applying the principles of forgiveness to our personal story with the explicit intention of finding relief from the symptoms of sickness, lack, persecution, etc. We have varying degrees of success in doing this. Frequently we experience an enormous relief as we surrender our old beliefs and reliance on judgments provoked by fear and guilt.

Inevitably, however, we find ourselves facing other fears, sometimes even a reoccurrence of those we thought were healed. This happens because the cornerstone of our story has not changed. We have altered some of its effects, demonstrated that it is *our* story, but have not yet changed it on the level where its real strength lies.

Separateness is the foundation of our perception and of the world we now see. And it is only our willingness to be free of separateness that will make any real change possible. The Holy Spirit holds the Vision of a forgiven world because for those who need a world, this is where change will first be most meaningful.

Our individual forgiveness triumphs will open our mind to what is possible, pointing us toward what is true. But we are all joined in a single mind/consciousness and there is no lasting or real meaning in changing "part" of a mind that is actually indivisible. There is no way to find lasting peace or happiness for yourself alone within a world where "others" still seem to oppose you. *Permanent freedom from fear and lasting joy will come when you see no part of your Self that resists loving, and no living thing that is not part of your Self.*

Believing what we witness day-to-day, forgiveness of the whole world seems impossible. Recognizing it is the intention for *what I want to see* that establishes the purpose of my vision, which then becomes the world I see, I can now begin to recognize it is only this old intention of separation I must forgive.

At the bottom of it all, it is our Oneness we must accept. The condition of our bodies or the "body" of the earth, directly depends on whether it is love or fear we want to find and share. Realization of our desire for the happiness of our friends and family is only possible when we recognize *everyone* is a friend and part of our family.

Practicing an attitude of Oneness with our forgiveness is a reminder that finding ways to come together is the single goal we need to have. It puts the appearance of our personal problems in a more meaningful perspective. And it moves us most directly to the experience of what Love really is.

Wholeness And The Truth Of Co-Dependency

We are inter-connected expressions of an ever continuous thought and completely dependent on each other to know the true nature of our One Self.

Learning now to recognize that we are whole is not just about being complete as a separate individual. It is seeing ourselves as an integral part of all Creation. No one who sees their self as a separate and different individual can feel complete because they are dependent on their ties with the rest of Creation *to know their Self*. Nothing that is a part of Creation can—in reality—even *exist* independently of the rest. Wholeness has no meaning if any part of it is missing. The fundamental nature of Creation is that it is whole and complete.

Within the belief that we are different and separate autonomous beings, everyone must feel there is something missing because the knowledge of what we are is inherent in our Being. However, our misguided guilt has provoked the *need* to be separate and distorted our awareness that what is missing is the feeling of being connected to the brother we are trying to be separate from.

Unconsciously, this is the basis for seeking personal relationships. The problem is, we look to partners to make us feel whole again, thinking they have something we do not have. What we find instead is only a reflection of our own feeling of being incomplete and unworthy. It is a principal of our perception that we find what we look for and looking for what is missing we *only find what must validate that something is missing.*

We cannot find evidence of our wholeness anywhere in the ego's perception or the world it has made. That is the purpose of the Holy Spirit and the Vision held There. The purpose of our relationships in the world is to find and accept that Vision for ourselves and then see it mirrored in others. It is to merge wholeness with wholeness for the microcosm and macrocosm must be the same. Every drop of the ocean must be all that the ocean is. The function of our practice of real forgiveness is to see the light that is hidden by bodies, not judge what they seem to do.

XVI

Joining In Purpose

"When brothers join in purpose in the world of fear, they stand already at the edge of the real world. Perhaps they still look back, and think they see an idol that they want. Yet has their path been surely set away from idols toward reality. For when they joined their hands it was Christ's hand they took, and they will look on Him Whose hand they hold."

T-30.V.7

Clearing the way to join is the goal of all our learning. Forgiveness teaches us there is no real reason not to accept ourselves or our brother. Choosing to abandon our need for separateness, we then can come together sharing the goal of forgiveness and use this union of purpose to more quickly and fully welcome what the "real world" brings into our consciousness.

"The Will of God forever lies in those whose hands are joined. Until they joined, they thought He was their enemy. But when they joined and shared a purpose, they were free to learn their will is one. And thus the Will of God must reach to their awareness."

T-30.V.11

To open our mind to joining, our purpose must be understood as a shared purpose that is in harmony with every brother, regardless of what his story may seem to be, even when his beliefs may appear to seek to harm us. When we have judged someone's thoughts or actions to be extraordinarily hateful, and are tempted to think they are so deeply immersed in hate and fear they couldn't possibly be ready to join us in peace, remember that the Holy Spirit is present in everyone equally, and at all times. No one is more than a thought away from accepting this Presence and the peace and love that are held there. And our acceptance of It makes it easier and more accessible for everyone to choose.

No one is further from the truth than their desire to find "a better way." And our choice to have it is the assurance that it is there. Together we are the "light of the world," but if there is anyone we think could not perform this role then we have denied it to ourselves.

> "The Holy Spirit was given you with perfect impartiality, and only by recognizing Him impartially can you recognize Him at all. The ego is legion, but the Holy Spirit is one. No darkness abides anywhere in the Kingdom, but your part is only to allow no darkness to abide in your own mind. This alignment with light is unlimited, because it is in alignment with the light of the world. Each of us is the light of the world, and by joining our minds in this light we proclaim the Kingdom of God together and as one."
>
> T-6.II.13

Within the awareness of Oneness, the idea of awakening alone is meaningless. That is only the ego's dream of finding a more "holy" yet separate self. Our goal is to remember together that we are One in truth. Joining in purpose is the most meaningful way to do this.

There is no place in any part of consciousness where any thought does not reach. It only takes a tiny part of consciousness that seeks the love of Oneness to affect and change the awareness of all the rest. While our mind connection is largely ignored, the influence that our thoughts have on one another is very strong. We all have had experience of knowing what someone was going to say before it was said, or who was on the phone before it was answered. That connection is more obviously observable than, say, a spontaneous feeling of sadness or unexplainable joy that has no "traceable" source. But traceable or not, any thought anywhere in mind will have an impact.

We have a tendency to acknowledge such thoughts when they fit with our beliefs or seem to answer something for which our mind has been seeking. Yet, because even now we share the only Mind there is, there are no "private" thoughts. Nor would we want there to be if all our thoughts were loving. But the point we are making here is that our thoughts do have effect throughout our consciousness, especially those that are loving, because love is what we all are looking for.

Our thoughts have long enough supported a world of suffering and hate. We have been ignorant of what is really true and of our ability to change what is not true. God's Will for us is perfect happiness, not sacrifice or penance. We can end the ego's journey of "seek, but do not find," and accept the means God has given us to share His peace and joy right now.

"How lovely is the world whose purpose is forgiveness of God's Son! How free from fear, how filled with blessing and with happiness! And what a joyous thing it is to dwell a little while in such a happy place! Nor can it be forgot, in such a world, it is a little while till timelessness comes quietly to take the place of time."

T-29.VI.6

We now realize it is not the world that needs to change, but only our perception of it and the meaning we have given it. We have it within our power now to change the course our thoughts have followed. We need not wait until there is evidence that there is a "majority" of us ready for this change. If it were not time to do it now, we would not have been given the means to do it now. We are the world. It is our story, in whole or in part, and we can change it as we choose.

Let us together forgive the world we have made and be witnesses to the miracles that will replace it. Together we can accept the Holy Spirit's Vision and give His promise of a world of peace a firm foundation in our consciousness. Let our forgiveness put an end to guilt and let what innocence has promised be fulfilled. There is a Vision of a forgiven world in our mind right now. It is a gift that was given us but will remain unrecognized and unaccepted until we have offered it to others.

XVII

"Justice" And The Goal Of Oneness

Nothing will change our perception or heal our world while we still find need to hold on to the importance of guilt and to pursue our separateness. And the ego's greatest practice of both unfolds in pursuit of its system of "justice."

Justice, in a world where there seems to be both good and evil, is what is needed to maintain a standard for protecting the innocent from the guilty. This standard is measured by attempting to match the punishment in equal degree to the crime or injury inflicted upon the victim. This, we believe, will be a suitable defense to prevent further victimization. In the ego's world, this justice is an essential attribute of every "civilized" society. But it doesn't address the cause of our conflicts and behaviors and so nothing really changes. The system of justice we now use is our response to believing that there are "bad" people out there doing purposefully "evil" things.

Our need for justice, as we define it, firmly denies that we are responsible for our lives and in control of what happens there. It unequivocally asserts our "right" to be a victim and justifies our need to judge—anything. It gives us reason to defend ourselves and "proves" that *our own* guilt is real.

Every thought that arises from the ego's perception is a judgment about something. This is true because its foundation rests on a judgment of itself. Whether judging or expecting to be judged, it is no surprise then that judgment is what we find everywhere. But we did not fashion our system of justice with this conscious awareness that it is we who have made the world to be a place of conflict and suffering and where we have a *need* for others to take the blame for our own imagined guilt. We have not allowed ourselves to realize we all are joined in our relationships each of us "dancing" in perfect response to one another's beliefs.

We do not want to see that we use what others do as a means to make our own guilt invisible. Whether it is genocide or a noisy neighbor, we must have someone worse than we to focus on and judge. We crucify ourselves in our brother's name and wonder why this "deterrent" doesn't prevent more war and crime.

Recognizing we have a choice for the kind of world we have, we need to reassess what our "institution" of justice really does and where it leads us. If its purpose does not bring us together or teach us how to love, it will accomplish nothing. We will not find safety by building better defenses and prisons to separate us from "warmongers" and "criminals." We are parts of a single consciousness making war on itself because of an old idea called "sin." And justice has become yet another form of revenge.

Fundamentally, every conflict we seem to "suffer" has come as an experience of our belief in differences that appear to separate us. What will heal our perception will come from our intention to join, not satisfying the ego's need to further isolate itself from everyone. If healing is restoring truth to mind, then justice must have restoring Oneness as its goal. And to this end, nothing can benefit one at a cost to another. You cannot feel the meaning of unity without knowing that when one gains, all must gain, when anyone loses, all will suffer loss.

From the perspective of separate minds, it is impossible to understand how the intention to exchange defenses for the desire to join can relieve another of their motivation to attack. Seen through the awareness of a shared consciousness, it is apparent nothing else could occur.

When you know that you "create your own reality," it is obvious that your intention for something pre-determines its outcome. Being of one mind, the dance we do with one another will always insure that what serves purpose for one serves purpose for everyone involved. How we now deal with sin and salvation, crime and punishment, has never achieved peace. It has not protected us from "criminals", nor done anything to eliminate crime. On its present course it never will. It is, however, working perfectly to achieve the goal *we have given it*—to preserve and protect the sanctity of guilt and the need to be separate.

To know the peace and harmony of Oneness, peace must be the goal and it must be desired for everyone, or you will not be free to have it. The thing you find unforgivable will be directly related to your own hidden guilt. Forgiveness must be blind to all the ways guilt seems to present its case. For there to be any hope of unity we cannot want for one to gain while another seems to lose.

When we look at the world's problems and see the goals of intensely conflicting interests present there, this would seem to be impossible to achieve. The desires and beliefs of the different sides would appear to be irreconcilable. But they seem to be that way for that is the purpose we have given them. Neither attack nor defense is ever really about cultural, political, social or religious differences. They all are a result of our common ego belief that there is something wrong *with us*. It is the thought of sin, and the guilt it engenders in each of us that we then feel a need to hide in our accusations and attacks on others.

We do not want a peaceful solution to our attack for that would thwart the purpose we have given it. And because defense is only attack seen and defined from another perspective, the principles involved are the same. No defense seeks a peaceful solution for then there would be no "bad guy" to blame.

A peaceful solution to any conflict is only as difficult as our willingness to forgive ourselves. When there is no need to project our own guilt, to have someone else to blame, we can want for our brother what we want for ourselves and there will be no basis for conflict of *any nature*. If this seems too great a stretch to believe it is only because we cannot yet imagine ourselves free of guilt.

The ego's first defense against attempting to become defenseless is that "you" would not also become defenseless and so it would surely suffer some loss. There is no way to logically appeal to the ego's perception why this would not happen. It does not yet believe we are joined in mind and consciousness. It cannot see that our desires and fears are the same for all of us. It cannot acknowledge that we move together toward the same goal, *regardless of what our perception may be!*

To know this requires that we take a step in trust. Forgive yourself for what the ego has condemned your brother for. Ask to see that what you want he wants as well, and feel the bond that comes to replace what you thought once was an irreconcilable grievance.

To forgive yourself means that you are willing to be shown that nothing has happened to justify condemning and crucifying yourself. You are not the body that seems to suffer pain and die. Nor are you controlled by the fearful beliefs that dictate you must defend against your brother. It means you are willing to find a peaceful and loving Self living in a part of your mind you have only dissociated with, but never actually changed. It means that as you let go the condemning thoughts that separate you from your brother, you free both of us and all the fearful world our unloving thoughts have made.

Whether seen on a personal or a global scale, the principle is the same. The child who takes another child's toy, the adult who embezzles a fortune, abuses a mate or even takes a life, have one thing that they share. The child whose toy is taken, the one whose money is stolen or is the victim of attack, also share a common bond. All of them, abuser and abused alike, dance together in a common belief. Each feels there is something wrong with them; all deny there is a Source of love they share which makes them whole and complete. In their feeling of separateness, they look outside for things or other people to make them whole. Each has an image of themselves shaped by the different meanings they have given their common belief. All, without exception, believe they are alone and are unloved.

They seem to meet as strangers doing battle over opposite beliefs, some seen on the side of "evil", others defending what is seen as "good." Yet all are dancing together, each in harmony with the other's beliefs to make their own story of differences seem real. The victim *must* have a victimizer to deny accountability for their dream of helplessness. The victimizer does not see they struggle with the demons of self-hate, and so must attack someone else to vent their hate and guilt. The dance is always perfect. It can be no other way, for there is but a single mind and consciousness that is the stage upon which all our stories play.

Several years ago, we were doing a gathering in New York City where we had also done one the previous year. During the first gathering, we had spoken of this dance we do, both in our close relationships and our casual encounters as well. We looked at how each of us accommodates the others beliefs and fears in an unconscious, yet very direct way. We focused on how we could open our minds to joining by consciously choosing to see the face of Christ and communicating this instead.

The following year, a young nurse told a story of how she worked the late shift at a local hospital, taking a nearly deserted subway home. She said she was always terrified, "knowing" one day she would be attacked. One night, her worst fear seemed to be realized. There was only one person, a man, sharing the subway car she was in and she was sure he was staring at her. She said that somehow through her panic she remembered our gathering and what we had spoken of and that despite her fear she really did want to see this man differently, and asked for help to do so.

As she exited the train, he followed and she "found herself," as she described it, turning to him and saying how frightened she was of being attacked and would he mind walking with her the short distance to her home.

She said they chatted only briefly, the way strangers do, but she soon no longer felt threatened. As she walked up the steps to her door she felt guilty she had mentally "accused" him. She turned to him and thanked him and then confessed that she first had thought it was he that was going to attack her. She said he looked at her for several moments, a rather puzzled expression on his face, shrugged slightly, smiled and softly said, "I was," then walked away.

It will likely take some time before many of us have the courage to do what she did under those circumstances. But what they both did is a beautiful illustration that we walk together in our life experience. And because they did do it, now it is easier for us all to do it as well.

f

No problem is ever solved if someone loses, for someone will then be without peace and *peace cannot be permanent until everyone shares it*. Problems solved with vengeance, or in any way where one will feel a sense of sacrifice or loss, will only reoccur. The form may look different, but the outcome will continue to divide us. Problems can only occur because of the belief that differences are possible. And solutions which do not aim at that correction will not solve anything at all. You and your behavior are not the same. This is an important distinction to understand. The image of yourself that we call "ego" is, however, made of bits and pieces of your past experiences; the manifestations of your belief that *have* determined your behavior. Believing the ego is who you are, it is now difficult to separate the two.

Your ego is an image, symbolic of who you *think* you are. And you will behave in whatever way best expresses what that image means to you. If you see yourself as guilty and unlovable, you will act in such a way so that others will seem not to love you. If you present an innocent and loving self to the world, you will find a world that loves you in return.

The defenses we use to protect ourselves from what we see as "injustice" are the very things that perpetuate injustice. Whatever the problem—be it a disagreement with a neighbor, protection of a child from abuse, or what seems to be a threat to world peace—all attempts to deal with it that separate those who are right from those who are wrong and can only make the problem grow because it is being fed with the same ferment from which the problem came. Mutual understanding begins with an honest desire to love.

We communicate with our thoughts, not our words, and loving communication breaches any defense of mistrust.

Those who choose to be unjustly treated as atonement for their mistakes are shown by those who do not judge them that love does not condemn. They see forgiveness does not mean sacrifice and attack accomplishes nothing. Now some doubt is raised against the certainty that they are "bad" and room is made for another way to see themselves and the world. Correction and change now seem possible because forgiveness has built a bridge between accuser and accused.

We will change the things we do by first changing what we value. We can correct mistakes without the need to condemn or crucify. They who have let forgiveness lead the way are free to see God does not judge them. The dance now can change, for without a victim there is no purpose for attack. They now can join in purpose by accepting God's justice of extending love equally to everyone. Now love has become the force that can make the outcome of unity certain. Healing has occurred because peace has been withheld from no one.

Every Child of God is evidence of His Justice, for all are given everything He is. No one is favored, no one is given less. No one can be omitted, for what is Whole can never be diminished. The perfect peace and harmony expressed by this perfect union is what we know as the Love of God. For there to be true justice anywhere, its aim must be the same as His: Give love equally, the same to all.

The miracle of real forgiveness

XVIII
Practicing Oneness

When feeling guilty, we mostly want to walk the world alone; privacy becomes a prized possession. That is the nature of the separated self. We avoid recognizing this because we gather to us family and special friends whose function is to relieve our ego sense of loneliness. But if we are all parts of an undivided consciousness, how can we come to know and accept what that wholeness *means* while cut-off from a part of our Self or while we look for peace or happiness for ourselves alone?

Can we remember that everyone is our brother while trying to make a better world without him? Can we know what being "wholly loved" means until love is all we want to give? While it may take a while to adjust to the idea of knowingly "taking our brother with us" along our path, it is an adjustment that finally will be made because that is what happens anyway.

Either guilt or innocence, lack or wholeness, defines the world we see and the path we walk. It is the same for everyone for we are of a single mind—in both illusion and in truth. It is not a matter of whether or not we go alone, but *where* we will go together.

The awareness of our oneness might well be lost were it not for the Presence of the Holy Spirit in our Mind being altogether unaffected by the ego's need for separateness. Everything that comes to us through this Awareness is a gift to teach us there is a way to find Light where now we see only darkness; to find peace where we thought there was only despair. It is a gift intended to unite what seems to be separate and so it will be incomplete until it is completely accepted.

The focus and the goal of all the Holy Spirit teaches is our Oneness, the wholeness and unity of all that has ever "lived." What is taught is nothing new, it is a simply a reminder of what has always been. And because Oneness is the heart of the message, *the message will not be fully heard until everyone hears it.*

This makes little sense to us now as we experience an incomplete and divided Self. We imagine that what the body encompasses is independent from the rest of what the ego can conceive. Having closed our mind to what it is a part of, we have lost the sense of what it means to be fully connected and whole. *We will not know what we are missing until the need to feel separate is gone.*

This realization can perhaps best be understood in the context of understanding the nature of Love. The ego's definition of love must accommodate its perception that separateness is real. It is given to some who are deserving and withheld from others who are not. It is used to satisfy needs. We love someone because they seem to bring us something we lack. It is used as a special designation to set one apart from another.

The nature of Love as it was given us in our Creation is quite the opposite. Here, Love cannot be exclusive or used to set apart. It expresses the intention of Creation to extend Itself with the assurance It will infinitely remain the same.

Love is the essence and expression of what Oneness is. Its true nature, the full impact of what It is, cannot be realized until It satisfies its function of joining what It touches, and touching everything It sees.

In the same way, we cannot "hear" the message of Oneness "alone." We cannot walk the path toward what is true, or try to learn of Love or hope to awaken from our dream while making judgments that isolate us from others.

This would be an impossible conundrum were it not for the Presence of the God Self in our Mind that connects us to the truth. This is our "bridge" from the ego's perception to the awareness of our Oneness. It is the Light into which we can bring the illusions of our darkness. It is where our every thought of sin is transformed into a *real* possibility to Love; where we can begin to experience the awareness of what Oneness is.

Not everyone seems ready to awaken to the truth. Most are not aware of what the truth is, certainly unaware they are the very presence of it. But there are also those who are aware. They still see the world and understand its pull of sorrow and of pain. But they also have felt the Presence of something else—a sense of freedom that arose when, for a moment, the fear of guilt was gone; when a sense of loving came to take its place and reminded them of something nearly lost.

This is the awareness the God Self holds. It speaks of what Love really is and as that feeling is absorbed, because of the nature of what It is, It must be shared. Just as Creation knows no bounds, there is no place where Love begins, nor can It be contained.

The instant this feeling comes upon you, you have become a teacher of God. It does not matter the form the teaching takes for it will be directed by the part of you that knows it is a part of God. What is important is not to deny the urge you have to do this. Bringing this awareness to our consciousness is our function. Doing this consciously is how we practice forgiveness, keeping our Oneness in constant focus.

The miracle of real forgiveness

XIX
Who Am I?

The Presence of the Holy Spirit and the awareness embodied within that Presence is in every way the mirror of what we really are. The only difference is there is no denial that It Is what It Is.

God placed this Presence in our Mind because of that—the lack of denial of what is true about It. It is not there to over-turn the ego's beliefs, which would only make them real, but to be the unchangeable witness to *what is true and real*. Truth needs no defense. Nor do we question it when our mind is not distracted by the ego's perception.

We now think there is an alternative between truth and illusion. While we do, it is necessary to learn to tell the difference between the two. This is the function of the Holy Spirit and our purpose here. There are principles we can learn to help us, but to get past the distortion our guilt imposes on our thinking, we need the clarity of the Awareness of our Holy Spirit—our God Self—to lead us.

The world is an illusion—a state of mind based on sin and separation which cannot be true. It is an attempt to distance us from God, keeping "Him" neatly tucked away in Heaven. But we have also made the world to be the place where we seem to experience the body-self that we have made. To simply let it go seems quite a sacrifice. We cannot yet conceive of being a "spirit self" that needs no physical world.

Upon learning that God did not make this world, the first conclusion the ego leaps to is that the sense of separation from Him must be real. He is not "here" so we must have been abandoned to our fears and helplessness. It is true that God does not "see" our world because it is made from thoughts that are not true. But God does see us dreaming of a world that blocks our awareness that we are a part of Him.

From its perception of guilt, it is easy for the ego to either believe that God does not care about our suffering, knowing it is unreal, or expects us to atone for the sin that we imagine caused it. Neither is true. We have *not* separated from Him nor lost His Love. That is only part of the dream. He is with us—we are a part of Him—whether in our dream, or free of it. It is only within *our* awareness, not His, that division and separateness can seem real. No matter how desperately we may try to *feel* unloved, *being* unloved is something we cannot bring about. We can deny Love's Presence. We cannot be free of It.

The world is an illusory state of mind, but there also exists "here" the awareness and the Presence of what *is* true. Accepting this awareness, adopting the way of thinking It offers in our attitude and the choices we make, we change our personal story of what is true. But not everyone seems ready to do this at once.

Time is the great deceiver as we weave our dreams along what seems to be an evolutionary path. But dreams exist only to accommodate our beliefs and time is needed to give a sense of distance that could seem to separate us from our eternal nature.

The primary role time plays in our awakening is to separate the moment of falling asleep from the one where we awaken. This ensures there will be different paths to follow and progressive learning to unfold. This, in turn, offers many opportunities along the way for the ego's perception to remain in control and find ever more ways to make the dream seem real.

Outside our story there is no time. There is no "moment" between sleeping and waking, no distance to the path that would seem to lead us from one to the other. Yet because our belief in separateness is so great, we have "pursued" our awakening slowly, in stages we could more easily accept. But the momentum of our change is growing; we can now accept what only a short "time" ago was unacceptable. And one of the things that will quicken our pace still further is to bring to our consciousness the awareness that the dream we seem to struggle to overcome, has already ended. We follow a path that time has made, but backward from the point of its completion.

Take a moment and envision what it would mean to already have reached your goal. Feel the release that comes from knowing there is no need to struggle, nothing to overcome. How much easier will it be not to judge or wonder if you will ever discover what it is like to be wholly Loved.

We can choose at any time to be free from our judgments, but imagining there was a need to first "make right" our sins, we justified the value of a path to get it done. But with that belief there will *always* be a path, a reason not to be free.

Consider this idea: You have never stopped being the whole and perfect creation of God. You are a part of All that Is. There is no guilt in you because there is no" sin" in Him. And what is true of you is true of everyone. Give this understanding some space to grow and free you from the burden of wondering how to let go of your beliefs. Give it a chance to become part of your forgiveness attitude.

XX

A Summary Of Applying
The Principles Of Real Forgiveness

The umbrella under which forgiveness is learned, the ultimate and final justification for it, is that what we judge is meaningless. In Lesson 240 of *A Course in Miracles*, it states:

> *"Not one thing in this world is true. It does not matter what the form in which it may appear. It witnesses but to your own illusions of yourself. Let us not be deceived today. We are the Sons of God. There is no fear in us, for we are each a part of Love Itself."*

What is true is permanent and eternally changeless. It is a joyful and complete sense of Being, each part depending on the rest for what it is. Because it is changeless, it cannot be threatened. What is unreal is the frail image of a self and a fear-filled world we have made from the impossible thought that we could sin, become unlovable and cut off from all that we had loved.

An overview of teaching, learning and applying the forgiveness principles could be summarized like this:

1. I first must be willing to acknowledge that whatever I see in the world that upsets me, that keeps me from loving, is my personal version of "there is something wrong with me and I cannot be loved." It is important as well to acknowledge that it is totally irrelevant what that "thing" may be because in all stories told of sin and separation, whether big or small, in their outcome they are the same.

I can prepare myself to more quickly and easily forgive by learning to see that what I have perceived as attack is actually a call for love. Every thought that seems to condemn someone else is a story of personal fear and pain. We never judge another for his "sins." Only for our own. Despite the momentary gratification of hiding our guilt behind what someone else seems to have done, if guilt rules my mind I will suffer all of it's effects. My freedom is as great or small as I am willing to free others from the judgment of our guilt.

As enticing as it may be to want to bring "justice" to the many forms of "holocaust" and "crucifixion" our ego stories pursue, not one of them will ever end in peace or point toward our Oneness. Attack eternally perpetuates attack. Forgiveness breaks the cycle and makes loving possible.

When what I "see" upsets me, I must be reminded there is something I am missing. There is a fear within my mind that has over-laid the Vision of Truth. There is another way for me to see. My only *real* choice here is whether I will continue to rely on the perception that has brought me pain, or ask for the Vision the Holy Spirit holds.

2. *Then I must decide: Do I want the manifestation of this story to continue to be my world, or would I prefer a loving, peaceful and happy one that I would find great joy in sharing with everyone else?*

This is the time to clearly acknowledge: *Are any of my grievances more important than being happy?* In clear moments this may seem an obvious choice, but, left unchallenged, the ego will want to assert that many grievances *are* obligations; that there is satisfaction, even happiness, found there. It cannot see that what it withholds from another is actually what it has denied to itself.

> *"Condemn and you are made a prisoner. Forgive and you are freed. Such is the law that rules perception."*
>
> WB-198.2

3. *Then I must admit without reservation, I do not know how to change my own belief, but I am willing to learn by surrendering—really surrendering—my story of guilt and judgment to my God Self because I do not want it anymore!*

This is a most difficult statement to make for, consciously or unconsciously, I have made my world the way it is because that is the way I think it should be. And unless I am vigilant and persistent in my determination to be free of them, my old habitual patterns of thinking will reappear by default.

4. *Now it becomes very clear that if I am to be free of what guilt has made, I must first forgive myself before I can*

release the others I have condemned, and it must be the Holy Spirit that directs my forgiveness process. It must facilitate my learning and my practice by showing me how to offer what I want to everyone. I will learn to rely on this Vision by teaching it to others. I will become a teacher of God.

This is the process *A Course in Miracles* describes as "teaching what you want to learn." It is the most effective way our ego will accept learning. To make it even more efficient, I will learn to recognize that what I had called "challenges" are really opportunities to find what I have not forgiven in myself.

I will be determined not to follow my old patterns and judge myself for how often I forget and fail to forgive. This could only be further evidence my guilt was real. I will learn to laugh at my mistakes (and yours) instead of judging them, simply because *they are meaningless!*

I will remember my Innocence is not earned. It is not something I even have control over. It is the state of Grace of my Creation and will forever remain as It has always been.

5. *I will take a moment now in the Presence of my God Self to feel my gratitude for this Gift God has given us. I will feel the freedom that has come in knowing I do not have to struggle with my guilt, reconcile or atone for it in any way. I can simply give away what never has been mine and free the world to peace. I will accept His promise that our innocence was never lost because His Love has never faltered.*

I am ready now to acknowledge God has not judged me, sees only Himself in me, and that His Will for me is perfect happiness. I am willing to accept the freedom that comes from my forgiveness, *regardless of how good it makes me feel!*

Freeing Yourself To Love

Guilt is a judgment we have made upon ourselves and the entire world that love does not exist. What we call "love" now is just a substitute for what it really is, a shadow that guilt allows us to accept. The enormity of what Love is cannot be grasped until you have forgiven yourself and spent a moment free of guilt. Only then will you begin to get a sense of who you really are, and for what Love really is. Then you can begin to appreciate what you have denied yourself, and all the world as well. Forgiveness truly is what frees the mind to love.

It is difficult to grasp how completely the meaning of what Love is changes when the perception of guilt is removed. I did not appreciate the magnitude of this truth until I had glimpsed the Vision of the real world I described earlier. Somehow, when in that moment, I was free of guilt and did experience a freedom that changed the experience of loving entirely. In that moment, *there was nothing else!*

It was not about loving someone or some "thing." It was not *about* anything. It was simply what I am and how I express what I am. It is what I have always been, but is now hidden by what in that moment seemed smaller than a grain of sand, a wisp of smoke—a thought called "guilt."

There really is nothing to keep anyone from seeing the Vision of the forgiven world. Some will see it in images. For others it will be a "feeling," a knowing that is undeniably true. For me, the process of "getting there" was one of asking to be shown, and trusting that it must then happen.

Please try it. You do not need a formula or a process. Just take the time and *want to know!* Why else would this Vision be held where we *could* access it? It is meant for us to see, to know there is an alternative to hate and fear; to be our inspiration, our miracle of real forgiveness! And be encouraged to know that as each of us accepts the Vision, it will be easier for the next one, and the next, until it can be clearly seen by all.

The miracle of real forgiveness

XXI

The Gifts Of God

Helen Schucman kept a diary of poetry she had written during the time she had been transcribing what was to become, *A Course In Miracles*. A book of this work was later published and called, *The Gifts of God*. There is a passage describing God's Gift to us and ours to Him:

> *"God gives the grace to give as He must give, for He must give the only way He knows, and what He knows is everything He is. Christ gives as He does, being like Himself. And nothing stands outside the gifts They give, for every gift is all-encompassing and lifts the universe into Their Arms.*

> *"Yet what of you who seem to be on earth, and do not understand what giving is because you have forgotten what love means? What gifts are there that you can give to God? My brother, there are many calls to you from those who lost their way and need your help in finding it again. It seems to you that you are helping them if you respond to what they ask and what you think they need. Yet it is always God Who calls to you, and he who asks your help*

is but yourself. Who is the giver and receiver then?
Who asks the gift and who is given it?"

p.124

The gift that God has given us is perfect, changeless Love—the substance of All God Is. It is a "forever guarantee" that nothing, no matter what it seems to be, can break the bond that makes us One with Him and every living thing. It is time now to accept His gift and return His Love to Him. We are the gifts of God, created from His Love, so that What He Is will always be extended.

We have forgotten long enough. The memory of God and who we are is eternally rooted in our consciousness, only waiting to be accepted and shared. The awareness of our God Self is now strong enough to be heard. Our function is to use and nurture His Vision by forgiving our world and ourselves. For those who can, to make a commitment to honor Love more than fear, to place our trust in Truth, not dreams of guilt.

Our choice now is to say "no" to every manifestation of hate and fear our world may show us; "no" to every mild criticism we pretend is meant to help. To let it be known we have put our faith in loving, not condemning the gifts of God. We will support forgiveness teaching us that wars will end when we find no reason to judge our neighbor or correct our friend; that famine will end when we find no lack in our willingness to Love, that sickness will not survive the end of guilt.

Our gift to God is to hold the truth of His Love, as best we can, in every circumstance. Forgiveness is the gift we give our brother, restoring the awareness of the Grace of God to both of us; trusting in a Love we yet have not remembered, but somehow know is all we really want. There will be times we seem to fail, but finally our world must change, for there is no hate or fear in the Mind of God, so none, in truth, can long exist in ours.

Forgiveness is an attitude that dissolves all our judgments of something being wrong in the desire to simply love. It is the practice of making loving choices to find the freedom and happiness that loving choices bring. It is a law of perception that we find only what we look for. Let us look for God's Creation in our brother, instead of what our misperception has tried to make of both of us.

The miracle of real forgiveness

XXII
Our Function As The Light Of The World

As we each pursue the elusive "truth" of ourselves and of the world, there is no one who does not wonder what their purpose and function really is. Jesus has said that forgiveness is our only function in the world. Each of us who pursue this function in the Forgiveness Movement will use forgiveness in the way that best suits our understanding and our own need to be forgiven. All are important and will be used by the Holy Spirit in accordance with His Plan, that we might share His vision of a forgiven world.

In *A Course In Miracles*, I am struck by how clearly Jesus explains how he sees us performing our function. He does this in the *Workbook*, lessons 61 through 75. If we were to look for guidelines, a curriculum of sorts, to teach us how to perform our forgiveness function, we learn it here beautifully. I will summarize these lessons by repeating the fifteen captions and highlighting the thrust of each, but I encourage everyone to study them in their entirety.

Lesson 61
"I am the light of the world"

"Who is the light of the world except God's Son?
This, then, is merely a statement of the truth about
yourself. It refers to you as you were created by
God."

This is the claim we must make to consciously acknowledge and accept our rightful function in the Holy Spirit's plan to see a forgiven world. It is not a statement about the ego image we have made to substitute for our true Self. It is about the Son of God who is learning to accept what his true function in the world actually is. It is a statement of our intent to let go of our role as an undeserving and unloved ego, and claim our joyful inheritance given us by God. It is the beginning step in acknowledging the power given us to help others find the Light within them.

"I am the light of the world," clearly denies the ego's belief it is a "sinner." To accept that it is true requires that you question every belief the ego has, for they have all come from sin's lament that we are "not good enough." It is an invitation to bring every guilty, self-abusing thought about yourself to the truth this claims about you, and accept God's evaluation instead of your own.

This is where forgiveness begins for, if this is true, what justification is there to condemn what is the Light of the world? Jesus obviously means there is no one who is not the Light of the world. If you accept that as truth, can the world of conflict as you see it now also be true? Accepted without reservation, this lesson becomes the foundation for an entirely different way to see. It accepts the Holy Spirit's Vision of our function here; undoing what we have made that has blinded us to the Self created by God. The practice of accepting only this as true is the function of real forgiveness.

With this thought, the world must begin to change. While it is not changing the world that is important, it is the world that has reflected the image of who we believe we are. And so to change that world, we must also have changed how we see the one that made it. Then, seeing ourselves and everyone else in a more loving way, we will become the Light in which the entire world can see the truth.

Another key element introduced in this thought broadens our role beyond just pursuing forgiveness and awakening for ourselves as an individual. It acknowledges our power to bring the truth to the whole consciousness because our "minds" are always joined as One. It is the way we begin to consciously function as a part of the whole Mind, beginning an experience of our Oneness. It gives our function a more real meaning and opens us to more directly understand what Jesus means when he tells us:

> *"True humility requires that you accept today's idea because it is God's Voice which tells you it is true. This is a beginning step in accepting your real function on earth. It is a giant stride toward taking your rightful place in salvation* (correcting misperception). *It is a positive assertion of your right to be saved, and an acknowledgement of the power that is given you to save others. You are the light of the world. God has built His plan for the salvation of His Son on you."*

Lesson 62
"Forgiveness is my function as the light of the world."

The idea of "sin" and the resulting sense of dividing God's Mind into many different and conflicting minds, makes the world a place of darkness. Here in the world of separation the Light within the Vision of Oneness has been lost. What would seem to separate God's Son from the perfect Love of his Father would also blind him to the joyful harmony inherent in joining with his brother.

Forgiveness does not accuse or condemn any unloving thoughts or behavior the ego refers to as "sin." It acknowledges a mistake in perception and answers it by extending love because it is only a seeming lack of love that prompts our mistakes. Sin is not a thought of God and so it is not real. Forgiveness, by not judging, affirms that this is true which makes a space for joining and thus becomes the light for recognizing Oneness as our truth.

> *"It is your forgiveness that will bring the world of darkness to the light. It is your forgiveness that lets you recognize the light in which you see. Forgiveness is the demonstration that you are the light of the world. Through your forgiveness does the truth about yourself return to your memory."*

Forgiveness does more than heal a relationship or correct a misperception. It nourishes an attitude of wanting peace and joy more than the momentary satisfaction of a meaningless insecurity. Jesus reminds us that forgiveness, *"merely looks, and waits, and judges not."* WB-II.1.4:3

We will all find great relief and freedom from our guilt as we learn to step back a moment when we are about to leap to one of our more petty judgments, seeing the thing we are surrendering our peace for in the "bigger picture," and recognize how truly insignificant it is when compared to what it costs.

Every judgment affirms that there is something more important to you than being peaceful and loving, which also then becomes your mirror to feeling unloved. God's Love is unconditional, without bounds or limitations. The same then, must be true of our love, and it is from this that we derive our real strength. Yet this is what our judgments deny, for if our love is real and is our strength, then what we judge cannot be real and judgment becomes our weakness. And every lack of willingness to love asserts that it is *we* who cannot be loved.

> "Remember that in every attack (denial of what is true) *you call upon your own weakness, while each time you forgive you call upon the strength of Christ in you. Do you not then begin to understand what forgiveness will do for you? It will remove all sense of weakness, strain and fatigue from your mind. It will take away all sense of fear and guilt and pain. It will restore the invulnerability and power God gave His Son to your awareness."*

Lesson 63
"The light of the world brings peace to every mind through my forgiveness."

We are the means through which the awareness of the God Self is brought to the world, which in turn brings peace to the entire ego consciousness. Forgiveness is our practice of surrendering the ego's goals to those of our real Self, making the Holy Spirit's Vision of a forgiven world possible.

As we learn to accept forgiveness as our function in the world, what we had thought of as "personal" healing takes on a much broader meaning. Not judging, changing our mind, handing over our thoughts of fear, will still be the focus of our function. However, now the meaning of what we call "our" mind will change to encompass the whole consciousness. Consequently, the gap between us that our bodies represent will become increasingly less important.

We are Spirit Beings and we will now begin to see that *without the thought of sin, our brother is like us in every way.* We live and function within the same Mind. We cannot change that and so even our ego consciousness can only be separated by its beliefs. We have the power to bring peace to every mind because all minds intermingle with our own and everyone wants exactly what we want, regardless of how they may show it.

> *"How holy are you who have power to bring peace to every mind! How blessed are you who can learn to recognize the means for letting this be done through you! What purpose could you have that would bring you greater happiness? You are indeed the light of the world with such a function."*

It is the Holy Spirit, the Presence and memory of our God created Self, that is unaffected by the ego belief that we are separate. This awareness bridges the gap that we perceive to exist between our bodies. It also bridges the differences in our beliefs of what we want and need and where our completion and happiness are. So when it is our desire to step beyond the boundaries of our perception and remember a Love buried deep within our consciousness, it is this Part of us that responds and brings that awareness into the space we now make for it.

Because there is no part of our consciousness that does not want the same Love we seek, the God Self answers every call for love with the gift of love that we have offered. This is the blessing of our Oneness and the power it has when we consciously recognize and call forth the means God has given us to replace our perception of being separate from, and deprived of, our brother's love.

We are "the light of the world" and will know it when we have brought it from its guilty hiding place in our mind and shared it with others in our world.

Lesson 64
"Let me not forget my function."

In our quiet moments or when enjoying the company of someone we love, being at peace seems such a natural and easy thing to do. And then moments later we find that once again we are engaged in judgment because what we think we want is being thwarted by that same person we felt so loving with mere moments before. This will be our experience until we claim responsibility for our thoughts, and remember that our happiness *does not* originate in the world, nor is it dependent on what others do or say.

We have made the world as a place to hide our guilt and while we give it that purpose we will also use it as the means to find salvation from guilt—a short step from thinking it is also the source of our happiness.

> *"The purpose of the world you see is to obscure your function of forgiveness, and provide you with a justification for forgetting it. The Holy Spirit has another use for all the illusions you have made, and therefore He sees another purpose in them. To the Holy Spirit the world is a place where you learn to forgive yourself what you think of as your sins."*

It is very discouraging to go from feeling very loving to an ego "melt-down" with little provocation. While we are transitioning to being Spirit-led and are determined to be free of judgment, these experiences seem to signal failure. Here we must remind ourselves of two things: our misperceptions run so deep they seem to come upon us with no conscious intent, and our primary lesson of forgiveness is to realize that nothing is truly happening in our story, even when we do forget.

Our consciousness tends to react blindly to every chance it can imagine to feel guilty because guilt is the basis for the image of the self that we have made. Our guilty self would tell us it is unthinkable, counter-productive at best, to welcome recognizing our mistakes as opportunities for healing. Yet it is these subtle, often intricately disguised beliefs that prevent us from establishing a real foundation for forgiveness.

How perfectly it will break the pattern of our guilty thinking when we are determined to remember only our loving thoughts and feel absolutely free to laugh at all the rest. To disregard guilt in whatever form it appears is our escape from illusions. How joyful it will be to fulfill our function then without the familiar expectation of what might follow allowing ourselves to be happy.

> *"The world's salvation awaits your forgiveness, because through it does the Son of God escape from illusions. The Son of God is you. Only by fulfilling the function given you by God will you be happy. Every time you choose whether or not to fulfill your function, you are really choosing whether or not to be happy."*

Lesson 65
"My only function is the one God gave me."

> *"The full acceptance of salvation as your only function necessarily entails two phases; the recognition of salvation as your function, and the relinquishment of all other goals you have invented for yourself. This is the only way in which you can take your rightful place among the saviors of the world."*

Since you first decided to accept that forgiveness is your function in the world, your ego will have more than likely been periodically rebelling—in ways both subtle and overt. What you considered your "advances" may seem to disappear. Forgiveness issues thought to be resolved reappear for "no reason." These are not failures, nor have you regressed. But forgiveness is unsafe territory to the ego's perception and it will quite naturally want to re-examine and resist such "drastic" behavior. Understand it for what it is; be secure in the Presence of your God Self to help you over the "bumps, and move ahead.

There is another block as well that could seem to thwart accepting the function given us by God. We have not idly accepted our belief that we must be separate from Him. We have kept our "guilty" brother between ourselves and God so that he would receive the judgment we expected for ourselves. And so the more we consider removing these barriers, the more vulnerable the ego feels. It is not easy to accept a function from God when it is God we have been hiding from.

It is important here to take some quiet time, reaffirm your forgiveness goal as the one that God has given you, and let all thoughts that might resist this now come up. Bring each one to the Presence of the Holy Spirit. Ask to be shown what its threat really represents to you and how, by accepting the function God has given us, it will be healed. This is our opportunity to consciously deal with the hidden feeling that there is some real need to hide from God, and to welcome instead the awareness that our will still must be joined with His. Be sure that you allow any thought to surface that would seem to indicate you want something else more than the function God has given you. Do this until you can earnestly say, *"My only function is the one God gave me. I want no other and I have no other."*

Lesson 66
"My happiness and my function are one."

"You have surely noticed an emphasis throughout our recent lessons on the connection between fulfilling your function and achieving happiness. This is because you do not really see the connection. Yet there is more than just a connection between them; they are the same. Their forms are different, but their content is completely one."

Until your happiness and your function are the same, sacrifice, however subtly, will continue to influence your perception. And as long as sacrifice is present in your mind you cannot understand the nature of what forgiveness is or what loving means.

Only someone who wants to be happy can truly forgive. Guilt and unhappiness are inseparable, only the degree of each will vary. Happiness, like love, each being an attribute of the other, cannot be contained and must be extended. Forgiveness is this extension. It comes from the recognition of our innocence, and opens our mind to the presence of happiness and love that the blocks of guilt have hidden.

It is important to connect happiness to our function and recognize both are given us by God. Coming from the belief we have somehow lost God's Love it is an easy assumption that some form of atonement is required before we could expect that He would want our happiness. You may not relate to this directly, but how many of us can readily accept that happiness is our unconditional birthright? And if there are conditions to deserving happiness, who else could impose them but the undeserving side of our self?

When we know that love and happiness is what we can expect from God, we will no longer be obsessed with trying to find their substitute from something in the world.

Lesson 67
"Love created me like Itself."

Until we have had the experience of feeling the peace and freedom forgiveness brings, it is hard to imagine that there is such a different way to think. When we look outward at the world and assume it exists "there" by some other means, and to serve some other purpose than to validate our belief, who would question that what we think we see is real? Or that there was an entirely different "world" that would appear when our belief has changed?

> *"Today's idea is a complete and accurate statement of what you are. This is why you are the light of the world."*

Our mind is divided now; there seems to be two parts of us. Both parts perceive everything to be like itself. For us to function as the Light of the world, holding the awareness of what is true, we must do so from the part that knows what the truth really is. This is the Presence of our God Self that will come forward when we choose to express the Love it holds.

> *"We are trying today to undo your definition of God and replace it with His Own. We are also trying*

to emphasize that you are part of His definition of Himself. If love created you like itself, this Self must be in you. And somewhere in your mind It is there for you to find."

This idea is crucial to accepting what forgiveness has to offer. Forgiveness is not just to bring peace to a troubled perception of someone or something. It is to reveal the Presence of Love now in our mind, and bring it to the awareness of our consciousness to awaken the Truth everywhere.

The ego cannot accept that we are already loved, let alone consider that somehow we are the Presence of Love Itself; a part of the very thing we have always searched the world to find. But we will know it is ours when we offer it to our brothers, holding the light for them to see this truth is also theirs.

Lesson 68
"Love holds no grievances."

"You who were created by Love like Itself can hold no grievances and still know your Self. To hold a grievance is to forget who you are. To hold a grievance is to see yourself as a body. To hold a grievance is to let the ego rule your mind and to condemn the body to death. Perhaps you do not yet fully realize just what holding grievances does to your mind. It seems to split you off from your Source and make you unlike Him. It makes you believe that He is like what you think you have become, for no one can conceive of His Creator as unlike himself."

Grievances are projections of guilt. They are the ego's answer to feeling unloved by finding a reason not to love others. They guarantee that we will always need to feel separate. They make the fear of God inevitable because all of the grievances we hold against others we will imagine God holds against us. Our whole world accommodates the image we have of ourselves. As long as we judge others we will believe God judges us. And as our grievances hold our brother guilty and apart they also guarantee that we will suffer all we wish for him.

We cannot begin to learn that we are "Love created like Itself," while we still harbor grievances. We cannot find lasting happiness while withholding happiness from *anyone else*. There is no Light in us while we try to hold someone else in the darkness of a grievance, no matter how "minor" it may seem. Forgiveness is but a sham while we think we can forgive a "friend" but hold a grievance against one we think of as an enemy.

> *"Shut off from your Self which remains aware of Its likeness to Its Creator, your Self seems to sleep, while the part of your mind that weaves illusions in its sleep appears to be awake. Can all this arise from holding grievances? Oh, yes! For he who holds grievances denies he was created by Love, and his Creator has become fearful to him in his dream of hate. Who can dream of hatred and not fear God?"*

Will you know that you are created in Love while holding a grievance against someone who is just like you? Can you know your brother is like you while holding a grievance against him? This only makes God's conditions of acceptance the same as yours, and you will be the one that suffers from that inconsistency.

Watch for the "little things," the subtle ways a criticism would attempt to elevate your perception to the truth. Let forgiveness teach that there are more ways to speak lovingly than to judge, more reasons to feel good about joining than to stand apart.

> *"It is as sure that those who hold grievances will suffer guilt, as it is certain that those who forgive will find peace. It is as sure that those who hold grievances will forget who they are, as it is certain that those who forgive will remember."*

Lesson 69
"My grievances hide the light of the world in me."

> *"No one can look upon what your grievances conceal. Because your grievances are hiding the light of the world in you, everyone stands in darkness, and you beside them. But as the veil of your grievances is lifted, you are released with them. Share your salvation now with him who stood beside you when you were in hell. He is your brother in the light of the world that saves you both."*

We are the Light by which our consciousness can "see" because our Vision is shared everywhere. When we are blind, we have denied our sight to everyone. The power of our commitment to join cannot be overestimated. Just behind our belief of all that seems wrong exists an awareness so peaceful and filled with Love that upon seeing it, the world must yield its fear and hate. Our guilt-borne grievance is all that hides this from our sight. Jesus says the veil of darkness our forgiveness can lift will free the world entirely. Grievances are natural to a perception that relies on guilt. Large and small, they are so common to our way of thinking, yet so vital for us to let go.

> *"Today let us make another real attempt to reach the light in you. Let us devote several minutes to thinking about what we are trying to do. We are literally attempting to get in touch with the salvation of the world. We are trying to see past the veil of darkness that keeps it concealed. We are trying to let the veil be lifted, and to see the tears of God's Son disappear in the sunlight."*

Lesson 70
"My salvation comes from me. "

"Salvation seems to come from everywhere except from you. So, too, does the source of guilt. You see neither guilt nor salvation as in your own mind and nowhere else. When you realize that all guilt is solely an invention of your mind, you also realize that guilt and salvation must be in the same place. In understanding this you are saved.

"The seeming cost of accepting today's idea is this: It means that nothing outside yourself can save you; nothing outside yourself can give you peace.

But it also means that nothing outside yourself can hurt you, or disturb your peace or upset you in any way. Today's idea puts you in charge of the universe, where you belong because of what you are. This is not a role that can be partially accepted. And you must surely begin to see that accepting it is salvation.

"It may not, however, be clear to you why the recognition that guilt is in your own mind entails the realization that salvation is there as well. God would not have put the remedy for the sickness where it cannot help. He wants you to be healed, so He has kept the Source of healing where the need for healing lies."

There are two vital points in recognizing forgiveness as our function. Since it is we who have adopted an untrue story that exists only in our mind, so it is we who must make the decision to let it go. God's Will and ours are joined in this decision. But God cannot relieve us of what He has not given, and it is not His intention that we are deceived by our story.

The Presence of the Holy Spirit is our assurance that we will not be deceived by our fantasy world. He is not "outside" of us. God placed Him in our mind as an extension of Himself to bridge a gap His Son imagined to exist. Our role is to accept His Presence there where the need for healing is and extend all that He brings to us to our brothers who have not yet found Him. The light that we hold for our consciousness is what He has awakened within us.

Lesson 71
"Only God's plan for salvation will work."

*"You may not realize that the ego has set up a plan
for salvation in opposition to God's. It is this plan in
which you believe. Since it is the opposite of God's,
you also believe that to accept God's plan in place of
the ego's is to be damned. This sounds preposterous,
of course. Yet after we have considered just what the
ego's plan is, perhaps you will realize that, however
preposterous it may be, you do believe in it. The
ego's plan for salvation centers around holding
grievances. It maintains that if someone else spoke
or acted differently, or if external circumstances
changed, you would be saved. Thus the source
of salvation is constantly perceived as outside
yourself."*

This thought solidifies our resolve not to let our ego's
perception of what is real—the way the world looks—deceive
us as we accept forgiveness as our function. The world is a
place of appearances, and the purpose of appearances is to
disguise the meaning of something we want to hide. The
ego's purpose is always to hide the truth of wholeness and
Oneness and emphasize the danger of joining. The way it
most effectively does this is to disassociate itself from what
is in its world, seeing everything there as if it were "outside"
or separate from itself.

Only God's Plan for awakening will work because it always
addresses and heals each misperception at its source—*our
own belief*—in the way most meaningful to each one. There
are many seemingly insignificant things in our world that

we accept as harmless, unimportant to changing our mind, and awakening to the truth. But our belief is one "package," with all our thoughts expressing and continually reinforcing it. We are not aware of all the thoughts that subtly move us away from peace; that make wrestling with a grievance more appealing than forgiveness. This is why it is so important to finally learn to ask the meaning behind *all* our thoughts and how they may best be healed.

> *"What would You have me do?*
> *Where would You have me go?*
> *What would You have me say, and to whom?"*

Lesson 72
"Holding grievances is an attack on God's plan for salvation."

God's Plan for salvation—our awakening to the truth—is for us to finally realize there is nothing but our *story* of sin from which to be saved. There is no reason not to be happy and filled with love in every moment. Yet, with each grievance, the ego insists there is something someone has done, or not done, that withholds our happiness and makes love impossible. This, as we have learned, means there is still more of our own guilt and self-judgment to forgive.

The ego's plan assumes that sin is real and "salvation" only comes when the price for it has been paid. This is the essence of most religious teachings where it is believed that God must have made this world. To this perception, suffering is valuable. Sacrifice and revenge are needed.

With guilt in control of our beliefs, grievances are "normal" in our life. Yet we know now that God's Plan teaches that sin cannot be real because the "crime" of defying His Will can only seem to be possible in dreams. Only if we were truly separate from Him could this be possible, and we are not.

Grievances are always associated with something the body does. A person says or does something to attack you and *"he betrays his hostile thoughts in his behavior."* Yet, focusing on the ego's behavior ensures that we will never know the person. It is only their fears and limitations that are expressed in their behavior, which, when supported by us, only makes our own fear more real and further attaches us to our own limitations as a body.

If we make God responsible for our world and our salvation, the body must also be part of His creation and His plan must then at least allow for pain and certainly end in death. If this were true, all our grievances against those who harm bodies would be real and forgiveness left without justification.

> *"This is the universal belief of the world you see. Some hate the body, and try to hurt and humiliate it. Others love the body, and try to glorify and exalt it. But while the body stands at the center of your concept of yourself, you are attacking God's Plan for salvation, and holding your grievances against Him and His creation, that you may not hear the Voice of Truth and welcome It as Friend. Your chosen savior takes His place instead."*

Holding grievances can only ensure we will not be able to see the plan God has given us to free ourselves from the fear and grief of our misperceptions. The body is not made by God and so has nothing to do with who we are. The light of Truth is in our mind, as is the Voice for God. We can forgive our grievances and free ourselves and all our brothers who still struggle to find the light within themselves.

Lesson 73
"I will there be light."

The power of our will, extended to us by God and shared with Him, is the only real power that exists. When exercised in its natural alignment with His Will, it is the force that extends Creation. When used in pursuit of separation, symbols of separateness arise in our mind that seem to be bodies in a physical world *outside* our mind.

When we acknowledge that we are beings of Spirit/Mind, it is obvious that what makes mind function, what inspires it to create, is our intention—another word that describes our will. In the ego's world, our thoughts all seem to take form, but we disassociate from their effects because they remind us of the guilt they represent.

The power of our will is not diminished when it is not in concert with the truth that is the Will of God. But when not in alignment with the Truth, the thoughts and experiences that are generated neither extend nor alter what that Truth is, nor have any impact on Creation as It exists. Thus must they be considered an illusion of the truth. Jesus calls a will that is not shared with the Will of its Creator, "idle wishes," that make only a "world of illusions."

Understanding the power of our will, however misguided, helps us realize why something that is not real can seem to be the truth. It also gives greater meaning to what this lesson has to teach us. *"I will there be light"* is the acknowledgement of wanting once again to align our will with the Will of God and bring the world we have made into closer alignment with the light of His truth.

> *"Idle wishes and grievances are partners or co-makers in picturing the world you see. The wishes of the ego give rise to it, and the ego's need for grievances, which are necessary to maintain it, peoples it with figures that seem to attack you and call for "righteous" judgment. These figures become the middlemen the ego employs to traffic in grievances. They stand between your awareness and your brother's reality. Beholding them, you do not know your brothers or your Self. Your will is lost to you in this strange bartering, in which guilt is traded back and forth, and grievances increase with each exchange. Can such a world have been Created by the Will The Son of God shares with his Father? Did God create disaster for His Son? Creation is the Will of both together. Would God create a world that kills Himself?"*

When we accept God's plan for remembering the truth, we have aligned our will with His. From here the way is clear. We have held the Light and seen our brother's innocence together with our own. Our wishes now have all the power God gave His Son to extend His Love and see that It has never wavered nor lost itself in dreams of sorrow.

The Light we hold will not sustain a grievance or allow it to distort the truth. The world is then released from its thoughts of pain and death and made free to pursue another goal. The hollow figures who seem aimlessly to attack and hide from love are no longer mistaken for God's Holy Son. The light we have willed allows us to see the truth about them.

"We will succeed today if you remember that you want salvation for yourself. You want to accept God's Plan because you share in it. You have no will that can really oppose it, and you do not want to do so. Salvation is for you. Above all else, you want the freedom to remember Who you really are. Today it is the ego that stands powerless before your will. Your will is free, and nothing can prevail against it."

Lesson 74
"There is no Will but God's."

"This idea can be regarded as the central thought toward which all our exercises are directed. God's is the only Will. When you have recognized this, you have recognized your will is His. The belief that conflict is possible has gone. Peace has replaced the strange idea that you are torn by conflicting goals. As an expression of the Will of God, you have no goal but His."

This is the thought upon which all forgiveness rests. It is the firm denial that illusions can be true. He is not saying here that between God's Will and what seems to be our will now, that it is only God's Will that is true. His statement totally discounts there can be another Will. It does not give any reality at all to the very existence of the story we are telling.

"There is no will but God's" sets aside every pretense that another will exists. This means that any form of attack, fear or lack has no meaning at all. There simply is no other Will but God's and so no justification for judgment of any kind. This is the decision we must make that will finally put to rest the idea that sin is real. Any notion we could be separate exists only in our story. Now the "slate" is clean and we are free to let another world arise.

Lesson 75
"The light has come. "

"The light has come. You are healed and you can heal. The light has come. You are saved and you can save. You are at peace, and you can bring peace with you wherever you go. Darkness and turmoil and death have disappeared. The light has come.

"Today we celebrate the happy ending to your long dream of disaster. There are no dark dreams now. The light has come. Today the time of light begins for you and everyone. It is a new era, in which a new world is born. The old one has left no trace upon it in its passing. Today we see a different world, because the light has come.

"No shadows from the past remain to darken our sight and hide the world forgiveness offers us. Today we will accept the new world as what we want to see. We will be given what we desire. We will to see the light; the light has come."

At any moment we choose, we can begin to think with an attitude of forgiveness. We can envision ourselves as a loving, peaceful and happy presence, free of guilt in every way. We can choose that this is what we want because this is what we were created to be. To make the outcome of our choice certain, God has kept His loving image of our Self in our one mind, held securely there by the Holy Spirit for just this moment—the time we could accept what always has been ours.

We do not struggle against a world that is opposed to us, but against an image of our self we have condemned. As I forgive the world, I will find no one who has not forgiven me. In this way will I know that they are a part of me. My brother, and all that seems to be the world, live only in my mind—God's Mind, where all creation is. This is our real Home and we now can know perfectly well the truth of what exists here.

We have been shown the thoughts that have distorted our awareness of what is true and given the means to forgive them, letting us remember how it was before our dreams began. And we have learned how to accept God's Presence once again to gently guide us Home. All this we have been given and is present in our mind. That is why we must truthfully say, *"The light has come."* For us, then, all that now remains is our acceptance of this Gift that God has given: Our choice to forgive will make this possible.

We were told at the beginning of our journey not to stumble or turn away when we came upon ideas we could not then accept. Given our perception, it was inevitable this would happen. But our learning was absorbed nonetheless. The awareness was "planted" in our consciousness for just this moment; the time when enough of our doubts and fears had been set aside that we could choose to be the light that forgives the world and the "self" that made it.

Such a moment will arrive for everyone. Not because they have "advanced" in their understanding, or have necessarily learned all their path has to teach them. But because they have touched that place of truth within their mind and somehow know there is no need to live in fear and hate.

The light has come the moment we are ready to accept what always has been waiting for us; the moment when what we want is more than sin and guilt can offer. This is the moment we can forgive the world that sin has made and open our heart to accept a world whose purpose is peace and joy. We can assert "the light has come" because we are no longer willing to live in darkness and know that we can trust that darkness has never been God's Will for us. The light has come because now we *want* to see.

Please do not deprive yourself of the full content of these lessons for they clearly show us what our function and purpose in the world is and provide the exercises that open our mind to accept it.

XXIII

The Forgiveness Movement

The Forgiveness Movement is a web site for those to gather who want to change the purpose of their lives and of the world we live in. We are turning a corner in our consciousness; coming to realize the ways of fear and hate are no longer necessary. There is an alternative we had forgotten; a way to find peaceful and loving answers to our problems. As we learn that our ego consciousness is a shared experience, we can come together with a common purpose to bring a greater harmony to our lives and to the world.

As each of us begins to practice forgiveness together, a unified network of shared intention is extended throughout our consciousness. The unity of purpose directly denies the reality of guilt's illusions and the need we have had to be in constant conflict. Coming together we can support one another choice by choice, changing our own experience of the world and awakening our consciousness to a different truth.

The Support Network
A mind set free of the need to judge has had the greatest of all burdens lifted from it.

The heart of the Forgiveness Movement is a Support Network. It is a joining to practice forgiveness as a means of illustrating that by changing our purpose from finding reason to blame to the desire to join, we will free ourselves, and others, of the madness we now find in the world. We recognize there are no insurmountable tasks in the world, for we have made it and it will be whatever we truly want it to be. The only obstacles to peace are the ones that we have imposed together! Together we can remind each other that our goals and aspirations are the same. We do not do battle with our brother, only with the guilty image of ourselves.

Forgiveness will teach us we have the choice of whether we will live by the laws of love or hate. Through our mutual practice of forgiveness, we will demonstrate that a different experience of the world is possible coming only from our willingness to change our mind.

Despite how the ego's perception may interpret the world it sees, the movement of forgiveness gains momentum every day. There is already a vision of the forgiven world in our mind. When we accept that we are now moving toward the truth we are open to accepting this vision. It shows us the alternative to the ego's perception when we tend to forget that we have the power to change what the world now seems to be.

Each of us has a special function to forgive the story of sin and separation as we have made it real in our experience. Together we can demonstrate that all the stories are the same, none of them more or less significant or compelling than any other. This is the greatest gift we can give ourselves and the world.

Every thought that denies the illusion of our guilt invites a miracle to happen somewhere in our consciousness. Although all forgiveness is self-forgiveness, because we are parts of a single Mind, the intention then radiates outward to anywhere it can be received. In this way, each of us has a very important role in bringing peace to our consciousness and our world.

Please visit the Forgiveness Movement web site and become a part of the Forgiveness Network. Join those who realize that world peace begins with the choices we ourselves make to forgive and be at peace. Adding your name is a commitment to support one another in the practice of forgiveness.

www.theforgivenessmovement.org

The miracle of real forgiveness

XXIV

In Conclusion . . .

Would you like to awaken to a world where everyone loves you? How would you feel if *everyone* who crossed your path was closer to you by far than your best friend?

Perhaps this seems too great a stretch. How about everyone in your neighborhood? On your block? Your thoughts still rebel. There are those who don't even know me, you say. Some are bound to disagree with my religion or my politics; be afraid of the color of my skin or the language I speak.

This is the way our ego self perceives the world and justifies maintaining its defensive attitude. But it is not how others think or feel that make us doubt we could be loved. It is *our doubt*, our judgment of our self which has, in turn, led us to look for reasons *they* could not be loved.

This is the cycle of thinking we are lost in. Everyone wants to be loved, but we have shut ourselves off from that possibility with our thoughts of guilt. Forgiveness can break this pattern of our thinking because it is the intention *not* to look for guilt! It is, in fact, the relinquishment of our belief that *we are guilty and cannot be loved.*

What would you be willing to do to make the world a loving place? For most it would be costly for it would require that we "sacrifice" what we hold most dear: We would have to stop judging ourselves. We would, (gasp) have to be willing to love ourselves! And, practically speaking, we would have to forgo our need to walk the world alone.

To see a world that doesn't judge you, you cannot judge yourself. This is what is meant when we say, the world is not "out there." It is your personal mirror. It smiles or frowns on you as you are happy or sad. And all your happiness really depends on is surrendering—forgiving—the guilty and unhappy "self" that *you* have made.

This self has been firmly fixed in our mind by the judgments we have made of others, not for their "sins," but what we perceive to be our own. And so it is *our* loving self that is uncovered as we forgive *them* for what we have judged ourselves to be guilty of. Recognizing this it is easy to see why every judgment we forgive removes another justification for us to be unhappy.

Our connection to others is symbolic of our Oneness. Our happiness and our connection to others is intertwined. This can't be seen or understood while we think that what our brother wants or needs is different from what will make us happy. We have forgotten that it is our connection with each other that restores our wholeness and it is the sharing of our wholeness that makes us happy! No one is happy when they feel alone. There is no fulfillment when part of yourself seems missing.

If it is a peaceful and a loving world we want, we must know what frees our thoughts to be peaceful and loving. There would be no wars, no sickness, no global warming or "natural disasters" without the thoughts that give them purpose and substance. Without the belief that there is something wrong with us, the world *will be* a peaceful and a loving place.

It is our belief in sin that has seemed to separate us from our harmonious and loving Self and turn our consciousness to hate and fear, to sickness and innumerable kinds of world calamities. This is the thought that has shaped our thinking and made our world, and to change them both this is the thought that we must forgive and change.

We are all responsible for the world being as it is because we all share the single consciousness that made it. We have made the world together because we are one self and so it will be together that we change it. Not by another version of our own plan, but by a Plan that God has given us. Our part is to bring His Plan into our conscious awareness by learning to see our brothers as He sees us.

Joining in forgiveness as a shared experience is an opportunity for us to work together to do this; to step outside the box of our individual stories and begin to see that we all share parts in the same story. It is not about healing an individual self, for healing is the recognition we are not separate and so it cannot be done apart from the ones we are joining with. To recognize the meaning of this we must begin to relate to who we are as connected parts of a single, whole consciousness.

To experience our connection we must begin to think as a "universal Self." We must recognize that what happens for one affects all. What heals one is healing for the whole consciousness.

When it is the intention of two or more to be consciously linked through the practice of forgiveness, a forgiveness network has begun. As we learn to accept that our ego consciousness is our shared belief, the need for a "good guy, bad guy" mentality can change. As we begin to share and practice the forgiveness principles together, the network effect spreads to all those touched by our practice. There will be different reasons for our use of forgiveness, but when directed by the God Self, all will bring us together and so reverse the purpose of the world we now experience.

Each little willingness to remember there is an alternative to thoughts of judgment frees the world of guilt to a greater degree. When forgiveness is extended to one with whom we have had a personal grievance, our entire consciousness shifts to a greater sense of harmony. In this simple way, every thought of forgiveness heals our consciousness and our world.

Our ego consciousness has been "evolving," moving toward the truth since the first moment we seemed to fall asleep. God placed the Awareness of Truth in our mind for the purpose of our remembering the truth, as we could accept it. This alone assures us there will be an end to dreaming. The time we will accept it, however, is up to us. Jesus tells us the purpose of giving us *A Course In Miracles* now is to save time.

We can do much to expedite our memory of the truth simply by our willingness to *look* for truth instead of following the ego's inclination to look for things to judge. A good example of this is in our determination not to see attack, but to recognize instead a call for love. As has been said many times before, we find what we look for because the intention behind our thoughts has already determined the meaning and the experience we will get from them.

How difficult is it to want to find innocence instead of guilt? It is as easy or as hard as it is to accept that what happens in the world does not affect the reality of who we are. How open are we to experience the miracles of real forgiveness? As willing as we are to accept that we are perfectly loved, right now.

Recently someone said to me, "Don't you think it's a bit ambitious, this project to change the *world*?" And indeed it would be if it were the *world* we had to change. But all we really have to change is the way we see ourselves and the world will miraculously change as well.

Let the magnitude of this thought really sink in: *Nothing outside our mind is forcing us to hate, to suffer and to die.* We can accept a different "self," and have another world. We can choose to let go of what we have valued in the past and share with everyone that there is another way.

We have all the learning "tools" we need. As unapparent as it sometimes seems, we do want to love and the very

Presence of Love is always present in our one Mind, to show us how to Love. In the beginning it might seem as if we are swimming "up-stream," but that will change as it becomes more clear that we are both the "swimmer" and the "stream."

We began our little journey here pondering what it would be like to go about our day with our mind filled only with happy and loving thoughts. Hopefully we now know how this can be possible. Through our use of real forgiveness we can recondition our thinking, creating a habit of looking for what is "right" about each other, and find our loving self in the bargain.

If you want to give welcome to a loving brother and a loving world, then start today by laying its foundation in your determination to see the face of love that surrounds you *now*, though it may be hiding behind a mask of guilt or fear. When this seems difficult, *remember that what you see is not in the world, but in your mind. And there you will only see what you want to find.* You can forgive what you thought you saw before and give the miracle of a forgiven world to everyone.

Our function within the world of time is one of learning how to "see." What we see now are images our mind makes from its need to disassociate and so separate from what it judges to be "wrong" about itself. The belief that everything is different and separate from us is the one thought that distorts all our thinking and hides the truth from us. The true nature of our loving and harmonious Self is turned up-side-down and lost in the big and little wars we wage to preserve the gap we want between us.

Our world is made of countless stories of countless ways we reinforce this simple thought. The history of our stories is predominantly one of winning and losing the wars and making new battles to fight. But there has also been another "movement" in our consciousness. It is our movement to the truth. It is more obscure, less understood, but consistently gaining in strength.

In the past we had not known that separation was the cause of all that we struggled with. We didn't know because we were not ready to consider there could be another way to see—the possibility that the guilty thought about ourselves simply wasn't true.

We obviously still struggle mightily with all the repercussions of what this means in our "old as time" belief system. But what we struggle with isn't true and so eventually, "in time," what *is* true must emerge.

Forgiveness is the tool we have been given to "undo" the need we have to judge the illusion of our guilt, in others first, for that is where we first proclaimed it to be. But as we free those we have judged, we necessarily free ourselves as well, for it was only our own guilt that was used to judge them.

There is an exercise that can help us change the way we "see." It is very simple, yet in the beginning we will want to resist doing it. The purpose now of our perception is to make our differences seem important and very real. We have made them to encompass every aspect of our world from skin color, behavior, and religious ideologies to "intelligence", language, and even eating habits. However you think of yourself, there will be something to make anyone else seem different.

The exercise is simply this: choose to "see" another person being exactly the same as you. Picking someone you struggle with obviously makes this more challenging, but what you can accomplish will also be greater. Watch as your perception carefully points out the many reasons you are different. Each time, remind yourself: this is a thought I have chosen that hides the truth from me. I would see this differently.

Consciously choosing to change our perceptions of differences is basic in learning how to forgive and find the willingness to join. We are the same. Our beliefs are the same though we make them seem miles apart. And we all *want* the same thing—to know that we are loved and able to love.

We are the same. Whether seen from the reality of what we were created to be, or from the story of what we have tried to make of ourselves, we are the same. Regardless of our many beliefs and how utterly different the experiences are that come from those beliefs, we cannot change that we are all created from the same Loving Mind as part of the same Loving Being.

All the ideas that come from a sense of being incomplete, thinking it is possible to be the opposite to the nature of what is whole, begin to lose their meaning. Whether guilt shows up as attack or the defense against attack, we can see it still is guilt that is the cause of the experience we all share. Yet, when I forgive the guilt I have projected onto my brother to make him seem different, the reasons to be separate go away. When I see that what I have judged him for doesn't exist in either one of us, there is nothing to interfere with the memory of our shared Oneness.

We are the same. And the moment that begins to dawn on us, the shift in the awareness of our consciousness grows exponentially. Look for this awareness. As you find it, it grows even more.

We have the ability to choose what we will see. When we join the ego's search for guilt, we separate from what we see and hate what we have judged. But if we will forgive and join with what we see, our hidden desire to love will surface and be fulfilled. And we will remember Who we are.

The Miracle of Real Forgiveness

The miracle of real forgiveness comes as we abandon the judgments guilt would have us make that have kept a "space" between us. With these thoughts gone, there is no lack; no loss of wholeness, no "place" not filled with love.

Now another "world" arises, free of all the manifestations that thoughts of lack and loss have made. With guilt gone there is no wish for pain or death. There is no thought to hide the Universal Will for peace and joy. We are free to connect with one another and remember what it is like to unconditionally love.

Our function in creation when not obscured by our story of sin and separation, is to be creators. It is to perform the function Mind naturally performs: to extend Itself as It was created, a part of All That Is. When it is your vision that everything is a part of you, Creation is extended for here thought finds no resistance or opposition to Itself. And what It then "sees" becomes the extension of what It Is.

Our Mind has seemed split between truth and illusion, but as the illusion is forgiven and is seen clearly for what it is, the power it had found in the darkness of the ego's belief is brought to light, and with nothing to support it, merely fades away. When we are able to ignore the appearances of the many different forms a call for love might take, seeing others, as the mirror of ourselves gets progressively easier. The idea of opposites begins to lose its impact and its meaning. The veil of separation begins to lift.

Our Mind was never really split, for what was created without an opposite cannot oppose its Self. For a moment in time we have had two beliefs. What we are calling "real" forgiveness is withdrawing support from the one that tells the world's stories about why sin and separation must be real. As each one is denied, the belief that has held us captive to fear is falling away. With this shift in awareness our consciousness grows ever more free of guilt.

Choose to be a Miracle

There is a question we each must ultimately answer. Am I willing to love and be loved completely? Will I surrender myself totally to peace and experience a Presence of joy that comes only from being free of fear of any nature? These are not feelings to be idly wished for at some obscure and future time. This is how we would naturally feel the very moment our mind is free of guilt. And the miracle of real forgiveness is that this moment is waiting for us right now.

It is the moment when making judgments have lost their purpose, whether they are mildly criticizing or totally condemning. When we are willing to love and be loved completely, there is within us the Means to see that this is already true. Nothing more needs to happen. The miracle waits only on the willingness to be received.

The witnessing to our willingness to be loved is to choose not to value anything more than being loving. In every thought, in all encounters, we can either choose to connect or to separate, to judge or to accept.

There is a loveliness, a light consumed with joy that is within us. But it is hidden now by our belief we are not loved. We say "yes" or "no" to the miracle that would make it ours with each choice to join or to separate, to offer love or judgment. Through forgiveness we can learn that we are now free to love and be loved completely. We can begin to experience the peace and joy that only we have denied ourselves.

Miracles come naturally when we forgive. They bring an awareness of what is true and beautiful, a promise we are eternally loved. When you choose to accept your brother as our Father knows him, *you have become the miracle of real forgiveness!*

Tom and Linda Carpenter

Appreciation...

is due for all the loving support I have received since the forgiveness book project first came to me. There have been so many—more than I can name here—who have joined in and held the loving space for it to unfold. They have made suggestions and given encouragement. I am so grateful to you all. I'm sure many have wondered—including me—if it was ever going to be finished.

My gratitude also goes to the following:

To our "Brother," my constant companion and inner guide, the real author and inspiration for this project as well as the "project" of my "life" here;

To and for Linda, my Holy Spirit, my partner and the part of myself that I can readily acknowledge I would be lost without, and without whose technical skills and encouragement this book could never have come into form;

To Sandy West, Bridget Thomas, and Annie Blampied for their most generous contribution of time and editing skills.

To Keith Bollman, my friend and technical wizard whose "no problem" attitude has been so helpful in creating "The Forgiveness Movement" website;

To Michael Watson, whose programing skills were so timely;

And for everyone who will ultimately join in forgiving our world and making it a loving experience!

Thank you!